MEDITATIONS *from* A PASTOR'S HEART

Spirit-Filled Sermon Outlines for Pastors,
Preachers, and Teachers of the Word of God
BOOK 1

Jerome A. Jochem M.S., M.A.

WESTBOW
PRESS®
A DIVISION OF THOMAS NELSON
& ZONDERVAN

Scripture taken from the New Century Version®. Copyright © 2005 by Thomas Nelson. Used by permission. All rights reserved.

THE HOLY BIBLE, NEW INTERNATIONAL VERSION®, NIV® Copyright © 1973, 1978, 1984, 2011 by Biblica, Inc.® Used by permission. All rights reserved worldwide.

Scripture taken from the King James Version of the Bible

Any references to Greek word meanings were taken from *Strong's Hebrew and Greek Dictionaries* which also is not copyrighted but is an excellent resource.

Any other references are documented in the context of the sermon outline.

WestBow Press books may be ordered through booksellers or by contacting:

WestBow Press
A Division of Thomas Nelson & Zondervan
1663 Liberty Drive
Bloomington, IN 47403
www.westbowpress.com
1 (866) 928-1240

ISBN: 978-1-9736-2878-1 (sc)
ISBN: 978-1-9736-2877-4 (e)

Print information available on the last page.

WestBow Press rev. date: 5/23/2018

Dedication

I dedicate this work to my beloved wife, Roxie and my children, Molly, Crystal, and Faith. I specifically dedicate this book to my grandchildren, Andrew, Dylan, Heather, Alex, Jean, Isaac, William, Sommer, Chaney, Dixie, and Zach.

I would also like to thank Margaret and Cassandra Stubblefield for their help in getting this book published. Thank you both for believing in me.

Preface

The Bible is an amazing book! It has so many levels of meaning that its content seems endless. I have been preaching for 26 years, at the time that I penned this book, and conservatively have preached at least 1,325 sermons. I have found it unnecessary to preach the same sermon twice since the Bible provides new understanding and insight through the Holy Spirit each time I sit down to write a sermon.

In this book, I would like to share just a very few of the sermons that the Holy Spirit has given me for my church. Perhaps you will find some of the insights and truths outlined in this book to be useful in preaching. Remember that these are sermon outlines and you will need to fill them in with the message that God is giving you for your church, bible study group, or home group.

I am a pastor who has been baptized in the Holy Spirit and so some of my sermon outlines point to the empowering and gifting that comes with this experience. If you belong to a denomination which does not teach the Baptism of the Holy Spirit as an experience independent of salvation, you will still find many of these outlines to be useful as you preach about the basics concerning our Lord Jesus Christ.

Finally, I pray that you will be inspired and made joyful by these sermon outlines. Several times during my 26 years of preaching and teaching, I entered a dry spell and needed inspiration and encouragement. Preachers, pastors, and teachers all get writer's block, and it is my prayer that these sermon outlines will help you through such difficult times. May the Lord bless you with new insight, aspirations, and greater faith in Jesus as you use these sermon outlines to minister to God's people.

Pastor **Jerome A. Jochem M.S., M.A.**

Table of Contents

1

THE LIGHT

Text: *⁸In the past you were full of darkness, but now you are full of light in the Lord. So live like children who belong to the light. ⁹Light brings every kind of goodness, right living, and truth.¹⁰Try to learn what pleases the Lord. ¹¹Have nothing to do with the things done in darkness, which are not worth anything. But show that they are wrong. ¹²It is shameful even to talk about what those people do in secret. ¹³But the light makes all things easy to see, ¹⁴and everything that is made easy to see can become light. This is why it is said: "Wake up, sleeper! Rise from death, and Christ will shine on you." ¹⁵So be very careful how you live. Do not live like those who are not wise, but live wisely. ¹⁶Use every chance you have for doing good, because these are evil times. ¹⁷So do not be foolish but learn what the Lord wants you to do. ¹⁸Do not be drunk with wine, which will ruin you, but be filled with the Spirit.¹⁹Speak to each other with psalms, hymns, and spiritual songs, singing and making music in your hearts to the Lord. ²⁰Always give thanks to God the Father for everything, in the name of our Lord Jesus Christ.* **Ephesians 5:8-20 (NCV)**

INTRODUCTION:

What does it mean to have the "light" within us? How do we understand what we are to the world since we are full of the light of Christ? In this sermon, I would like to talk about the significance of having the bright light of Christ within us individually and as the church.

TURNING ON THE LIGHT:

In the beginning, God first made the light (Genesis 1:3-5). God then separated the light from the darkness, making two forms of creation and two symbols of kingdom rule.

- God's kingdom is known as the kingdom of light, while Satan's kingdom is known as the kingdom of darkness.

- He did the same during the creation of his spiritual kingdom. He first established Christ as the light. *In him there was life, and that life was the light of all people. ⁵The Light shines in the darkness, and the darkness has not overpowered it.* **John 1:4-5 (NCV)**
- Then Jesus brought forth God's kingdom on earth through his ministry and death on the cross.

LIGHT DIMINISHED:

What happens to the world when you turn down the light? We live in a dark world, but think how much darker it would be if the church were not here – if we could not turn on the light by our witness about Christ.

- Hate would increase.
- Violence would escalate.
- Religion would be even more corrupted.
- The government would be tyranny.
- Class separation would increase.

WHEN THE LIGHT SHINES:

What happens when the light shines brightly? There are direct and beautiful results from allowing the light to illuminate the world. These results are:

- Goodness: Kindness and a caring tolerance. Not agreement pressured by conformity, but a lack of negative and hostile judgment
- Truth: Spiritual truth integrated with love, but not love used as an excuse for sinful behavior. There is the love of truth and truth in love.
- The exposure of darkness: There is no confusion between good and evil. Good is not considered evil, and evil is not considered good.
- Removal of darkness: Evil, when exposed to the truth, is called evil with no exceptions! Steps are taken to remove evil from the world scene.

THE WAY OF THE LIGHT:

How do we cultivate the light in our lives and our culture? There are distinct steps that we can take to ensure that the light burns brightly in both.

- We are careful of how we live so that we live in the light and reject the darkness. (Vs.15)
- Show wisdom (thought) and take every opportunity to witness about the Lord. (Vs.16)
- Understand the Lord's will. (Vs.17)
- Do not get drunk to avoid emotional pain or relieve tension. We do not attempt to gain strength by using drugs. Addiction will inevitably dim the brightest light.
- We must be filled with the Holy Spirit because strength, peace, power, and security come from him, and that means we must allow him to empower our witness. (Vs. 18)

EXPRESSIONS OF THE LIGHT:

The light is expressed by what we do as we worship, and fellowship with the Lord as well as each other. By sharing the light, we encourage others to stay strong in the light. These expressions include:

- Help (speak to) one another with psalms, hymns, and spiritual songs. (Vs. 19).
- Sing and make music in your heart to the Lord. (Vs. 19).
- Always give thanks to God for everything. (Vs. 20).
- Submit to one another out of reverence for Christ.

CHILDREN OF THE LIGHT:

8For you were once darkness, but now you are light in the Lord. Live as children of light.... (Vs. 8)

Since each Christian has the light of Christ who is the light of the world, the church is filled with light. We are the light because:

- We once were part of the darkness because our spirits were unsaved and we were in the image of evil. We were in a night that was getting ever darker
- Now we have the light of Christ in us. Our dark spirit got replaced when we got born again into the image of Jesus.

That makes us the light of the world just as he is the light of the world

CONCLUSION:

Every Christian is a light that the world must see. The church should be a light to every nation. We must make an effort to burn brightly despite the darkness that surrounds and may threaten us. We must brightly burn as we represent the light of the world, Jesus Christ.

NOTES:

2

OUR FRIEND JESUS

Text: *¹⁴You are my friends if you do what I command you. ¹⁵I no longer call you servants, because a servant does not know what his master is doing. But I call you friends, because I have made known to you everything I heard from my Father.* **John 15:14-15 (NCV)**

INTRODUCTION:

One of the unique aspects of Christianity is that Jesus is not only our Lord, but he is also our friend. His friendship is by his own declaration and is not a religious myth, but a spiritual reality that all Christians can experience. In this sermon, I would like to talk about Jesus, our friend.

SIX CHARACTERISTICS OF A FRIEND:

Friends have characteristics that are universal, that is, all friends share these characteristics:

1. A friend is willing to sacrifice for you.
2. A friend is willing to share with you.
3. A friend is willing to stand by you in troubled times.
4. A friend is willing to accept you as you are.
5. A friend is willing to be loyal to you and expects loyalty from you.
6. A friend is willing to give unconditionally.

WILLING TO SACRIFICE:

It is of vital importance to know that the sacrifice Jesus made was because of love and not because of obligation.

- Jesus is an example of a loving sacrifice because he gave his all for our salvation.
- Jesus sacrificed his whole being, that is, his body, spirit, and mind, for our salvation.
- Such sacrifice defines Christian love as being sacrificial love.
- We may not be asked to give our lives in sacrifice for others, but indeed we will be asked to make minor sacrifices to demonstrate his love for people, and our love for them as well.
- An unwillingness to give or sacrifice ourselves for the sake of others is a sign of little or weak love.

WILLING TO SHARE:

Christ shared the heart of the Father and anyone who accepted became his friend.

- In this situation, the basis of friendship is our sharing a specialized knowledge about God.
- That knowledge was mainly about the love of the Father for his son and for those who would believe in Jesus.
- So, salvation becomes a basis for friendship.
- All those saved through Jesus Christ are friends, not only with Christ and the Father but also with each other.
- The principal arbitrator of the friendship that we have between God and ourselves and with each other is the Holy Spirit

WILLING TO STAND:

Love is devoid of judgment and condemnation. In our text, Jesus is clear that he wants us to support each other and encourage each other

- All of us will have "troubled times," and so we all need the support of our Christian brothers and sisters.
- Supporting each other is a significant function of the church as a community of believers who are expressing friendship and love for each other.

WILLING TO ACCEPT:

God's primary desire is to be your friend.

- Notice that he is willing to reach out to the lost through Jesus Christ for the sole purpose of friendship.
- In this sense, every born-again and Spirit-filled Christian is a "chosen one," because of God's desire for a relationship.
- Even though God chooses us, we can reject his choice by continuing to live a lifestyle of sin.
- In other words, God is a friend to a sinner, but a sinner is not necessarily a friend to God.
- There is a deep satisfaction in the knowledge that the love of God is so great that he chooses us to be his friends and will choose our lost friends as well.

WILLING TO BE LOYAL:

Keep in mind that friendship is God's expression of his loyalty to us.

- The idea that we will be loyal and obedient to God is the foundation of his friendship.
- God gives us a choice to continue in friendship with him by being obedient to his commands.
- Please remember that his commands are not burdensome, but mainly consists of loving God and loving our neighbor.
- It is true however that if we choose to continue to live a lifestyle of sin, we are simultaneously rejecting our friendship with God.
- To be a friend of God essentially means we defer to his will and purposes.
- It should not surprise us that God is loyal to us and he expects us to be faithful to him.

WILLING TO SUPPORT:

And I gave you this work: to go and produce fruit, fruit that will last. Then the Father will give you anything you ask for in my name. **John 15:16 (NCV)**

The second part of this Scripture is used to promote a false prosperity message.

- This Scripture does not say that the Father will support you regardless of what you are doing.

- This Scripture does say that if you are following his will and bearing fruit for his kingdom, then he will provide anything that you need.
- This Scripture assures us that God is not only a personal friend but a ministry partner willing to support us in the endeavor he designates for us.
- The first part of fulfilling the Scripture is to understand the will of God.
- The second part of this Scripture involves asking God for our ministry needs and depending on him for provision.
- Given our friendship with him regarding ministry, we can expect his unconditional support to help us fulfill his purposes and his will in our lives and the world.

CONCLUSION:

In every way, Jesus has shown himself to be our friend. It is to his friendship that we appeal when our lives take a turn for the worst. Remember, it takes two to be friends, and we need to do everything in our power to maintain his fellowship with us. In the last analysis, we need to love God, and each other and Jesus is our lifelong friend.

NOTES:

3

SALVATION

Text: *⁹If you use your mouth to say, "Jesus is Lord," and if you believe in your heart that God raised Jesus from the dead, you will be saved.* **Romans 10:9 (NCV)**

⁶Human life comes from human parents, but spiritual life comes from the Spirit.⁷Don't be surprised when I tell you, 'You must all be born again.' **John 3:6-7 (NCV)**

INTRODUCTION:

It is not possible to be a competent witness for Jesus without understanding salvation. Salvation is a mystery to many people because they do not know what it is, what it does, and how to obtain it. Instead, some people claim to be saved, have no idea why they need salvation, and try to be saved by any means other than accepting Jesus. In this sermon, I want to talk about salvation and some of its most critical ramifications.

THE MEANING OF SALVATION:

The Greek word for salvation is "Soteria," which means deliverance, preservation, and salvation. Salvation is the preservation from destruction, spiritual failure or evil. It means that you are born into the kingdom of God and that you can have a relationship with God through Christ.

SALVATION FROM WHAT?

- The penalty of sin by being justified. We are declared righteous. (John 3:16-17)

- Power of sin by being sanctified. We are set apart to God and free of bondage to anything or anyone.
- The presence of sin by being glorified. A future condition in which we live in the splendor of God forever.

CHARACTERISTICS OF THE LOST:

Lost people share some characteristics generated by their "lost" spiritual status. Sometimes, recognition of the negative attitudes and correlated actions can motivate a person to accept Jesus. Some of these attitudes and actions are:

ATTITUDES	ACTIONS
Disillusionment	Attention getting
Emptiness	People pleaser
Lack of Fulfillment	Compulsiveness
Lack of peace	Dependency
Loneliness	Self-centered
Restlessness	Fleshly behavior

COMMON WITNESSING MISTAKES:

When we witness to the lost, we can make mistakes which invalidate what we are saying or trying to tell the person about salvation. These mistakes should be avoided as much as possible by eliminating them from our style of witnessing. These mistakes are:

- Assuming a person is saved or understands Biblical salvation.
- Getting sidetracked.
- Trying to push the person into salvation.
- By offering only "fire insurance." We focus on avoiding hell instead of a relationship with God.
- By offering only a "ticket to heaven." A narrow focus on rewards rather than service.
- Failing to tell them about the cost of obedience. Stressing the benefits without the cost.
- Feeling personally responsible for another person's salvation.

SOME BARRIERS TO SALVATION:

Not only can we make mistakes in witnessing, but the person we are trying to reach may have barriers which prevent committing to the Lord. Some of these barriers are:

- Rejecting salvation over a lifetime builds the habit of refusing the message of salvation. The older a person, then the more he has denied the Word, and the pattern of rejection becomes stronger, so the message falls on deaf ears.
- People believe that they can't know if they have eternal life, even if Scripture assures them that if they believe in Jesus, then they are bound for heaven. (1 John 5:13)
- They think that Jesus never claimed to be God. (John 14:9-10, John 10:30)
- They believe that there are many ways to God and so a commitment to Christ is not needed if they practice some other religion. (John 14:6-7)
- They think that the church is full of hypocrites and so salvation seems worthless.

DOUBTS ABOUT BEING ABLE TO BE SAVED:

Self-image and identity will play a role in whether a person can accept salvation. Some of the attitudes and false beliefs that keep a person from receiving salvation are;

- God would never accept me because of what I have done. To witness to these people, focus on what Christ has done for that person.
- I can't give up my sin! To witness to these people, tell them that Christ living in them is stronger than the power of sin. (John 8:36)
- Committed the unpardonable sin! To witness to these people, show them that Christ's sacrifice is complete. (Romans 10:13)
- I need to clean up my life first. To witness to these people, explain that this is not possible without coming to Christ. (Ephesians 2:5)
- I want to become a Christian, but I don't want to make the decision now. To witness to these people, explain that no decision is a decision.

Jerome A. Jochem M.S., M.A.

ABOUT SURRENDERING:

12But to all who did accept him and believe in him he gave the right to become children of God. **John 1:12 (NCV)**

Many people do not know how to surrender to Christ! Some ways of surrendering include:

- Accept God's grace and reject works as a means to gain God's approval. (Ephesians 2:8-9)
- Give Christ control and live by following his lead. (Matthew 16:24-26)

BENEFITS OF SALVATION:

One way of helping a person accept salvation is to tell him about the spiritual benefits of salvation.

- You are completely forgiven and cleansed of all your sins. (1 John 1: 9)
- You are a new creation. (2 Corinthians 5:17)
- You are declared righteous by God because the old life is gone. (2 Corinthians 5:17)
- You have the gift of eternal life.
- You have the Holy Spirit living in you to overcome sin and to love others.
- God no longer condemns you. (Romans 8:1)
- Separation from God's love ends. (Romans 8:38-39)

CONCLUSION:

A person does not have to be a rocket scientist to find salvation. The message is simple, and yet, many people struggle with it because they do not understand or hear the message. Those who witness must be persistent and listen before they testify. By answering questions and relieving fears, they may pave the way to salvation.

NOTES:

4

GOD'S TOUCH - ABIDE THROUGH WORSHIP

Text: *⁴Abide in me, and I in you. As the branch cannot bear fruit of itself, except it abide in the vine; no more can ye, except ye abide in me.* **John 15:4 (KJV)**

INTRODUCTION:

As Christians mature in their walk with Jesus, many desire to have a close, intense, personal relationship with him. This desire becomes a strong drive to experience more of Jesus through the work of the Holy Spirit. After all, it is one of the primary purposes of the Holy Spirit to reveal Jesus to believers. (John 15:26, 16:14) Often, the Holy Spirit will show us Jesus through the anointing power that can be experienced directly by a believer, especially one baptized in the Holy Spirit. In this sermon series, I would like to outline the three conditions that must be in place to have a supernatural experience that reveals Jesus through the anointing power of the Holy Spirit. In this specific sermon, I will talk about abiding through worship of the Lord.

WHAT DOES ABIDING MEAN?

The older translations of the New Testament use the word "abiding." The more modern versions use phrases which give meaning to the word abiding. For example, John 15:4 is translated differently from the King James Version as follows:

- The New Century Version and the New International Version say *⁴Remain in me, and I will remain in you.*
- The Contemporary English Version says: *⁴Stay joined to me, and I will stay joined to you.*

All these translations imply that "to abide" means more than having an intellectual or conceptual idea about Jesus. These interpretations suggest that abiding in Christ is to have a living, personal, and emotional relationship with him.

SCRIPTURAL ABIDING:

There are two scripturally outlined ways to abide in Christ:

1. Through his commands: *¹⁰If ye keep my commandments, ye shall abide in my love; even as I have kept my Father's commandments, and abide in his love.* **John 15:10 (KJV)**
2. Through his love: *⁹As the Father hath loved me, so have I loved you: continue ye in my love.* **John 15:9 (KJV)**

Of the two ways mentioned above, remaining in God's love is perhaps the most powerful way of having a personal experience with Jesus Christ through the Holy Spirit.

- This kind of experience is personal because it involves an actual emotional involvement with God through Christ.
- Through the grace of the Lord and by the power of the anointing of the Holy Spirit, we can experience the emotion of divine love for us that is revealed by Christ for believers.
- The Holy Spirit's anointing comes through as we worship Jesus. In this case, worship becomes a personal and powerful means of abiding in Christ emotionally.

THE EMOTIONAL EXPERIENCE OF CHRIST:

One of the joys of being a Christian is to be able to experience the love of Christ. His love is an experience that goes beyond an idealized concept or just an intellectual knowledge. In other words, the love of Jesus enables us to know Jesus personally and not just to intellectually know about Jesus. The love of Christ becomes a standard upon which we live and which we judge the world. Once again, this is a personal experience which happens under the authorship of the Holy Spirit and is part of what he has been tasked to do in the world. The question is how do we achieve this emotional and personal experience?

THE FIRST STEP IS WORSHIP:

Although worship is a complicated subject, we can learn to abide in Christ through two types of worship. Both these kinds of worship have been in the church from the beginning, but the purpose of each type of worship is different. The first sort of worship is what I call testimony centered worship. The second kind of worship is what I call God-centered worship.

TESTIMONY CENTERED WORSHIP:

Testimony centered worship stresses the experience of the believer in relationship to the actions of the Lord. Through the lyrics and music, the worshipper emphasizes what God has done for him in his life or the lives of others.

- Testimony centered worship carries with it a message about what God can do or has done for the individual in a wide variety of situations.
- Testimony centered worship may include references to self even more than it contains references to God. That is, there may be many references to "I" and fewer references to "God."
- Testimony centered worship can be a powerful evangelistic tool because it declares the need for God in the individual's life. However, it may not produce a personal experience with God through the anointing of the Holy Spirit.

GOD-CENTERED WORSHIP:

God-centered worship is worship that exalts and focuses on God rather than the individual worshiper.

- God-centered worship concentrates on the character and qualities of God without reference to the emotional needs or circumstance of those worshiping. There are fewer references to "I" and more references to "God."
- God-centered worship unlocks the worshiper's heart and mind to both God's love and his power.
- God-centered worship lifts the worshiper into heavenly realms where he is more sensitive and emotionally responsive to God.

- God-centered worship establishes a bridge between the natural universe and the supernatural world. During God-centered worship, heaven and earth merge into one.
- It is during God-centered worship that the believer starts to feel the flow of power to him from the Holy Spirit.

CONCLUSION:

It is during God-centered worship that we truly begin to abide emotionally and even physically in the presence of God. The more intensely we abide in him, the more likely that the Holy Spirit will be able to work miracles in our lives. This abiding under the anointing of the Holy Spirit is the only thing which will satisfy the desire of the believer to have a deeper relationship with Jesus Christ through the Holy Spirit

NOTES:

5

GOD'S TOUCH - ACCEPT HIS POWER

Text: *⁴⁵Then Jesus said, "Who touched me?" When all the people said they had not touched him, Peter said, "Master, the people are all around you and are pushing against you." ⁴⁶But Jesus said, "Someone did touch me, because I felt power go out from me."* **Luke 8:45-46 (NCV)**

INTRODUCTION:

To me, it is incredible that people want to experience God's love, mercy, and compassion, but react with fear when they encounter his supernatural power. People accept the power of the Word, the power of the cross, but will run from the manifestations of the power of the Holy Spirit. This fear seems to be an instinctive response to the overwhelming glory that is part of the presence of the Lord. In response to this concern, with great reassurance, Jesus said: *"Have courage! It is I. Do not be afraid."* **Matthew 14:27b (NCV)**

When the Holy Spirit begins to show forth the power of God, it is very easy to reject the experience of that power because of fear. We eliminate fear as we grow in our understanding of God's power and begin to trust him. We can accept the power of God to the extent that we trust it. In this sermon, I want to examine God's power and instill a sense of trust that his power should be accepted so it can work within us as God so desires.

POWER:

In the Greek, the word translated as power in Luke 8 is "Dunamis" which means a force or mighty (wonderful) work. We get the word dynamite from this Greek word, and this gives us an illustration as to how God releases power during a church service. There are three elements needed for a spiritual explosion to take place:

1. Fire – Spiritually, our passion for experiencing the Lord's power is the fire. The greater the desire and the more determined we are to experience the power of God, the hotter the fire. This spiritual fire ignites the fuse. Fear, apathy, and anti-Spirit religious tradition are a few things that will put out the fire by quenching the Holy Spirit.

2. Fuse – Spiritually, the fuse is God-centered worship. Worship brings us closer and closer to the release of God's power and presence. Distractions and self-centeredness will put out the fuse.

3. Dynamite – The release of explosive power will take place when the fuse reaches the dynamite. In the same manner, when worship brings us into the commanding presence of God, the Holy Spirit releases his power.

PURPOSE:

8But when the Holy Spirit comes to you, you will receive power. You will be my witnesses—in Jerusalem, in all of Judea, in Samaria, and in every part of the world. **Acts 1:8 (NCV)**

Keep in mind that God releases his power for a distinct purpose. Every single manifestation of that energy produced by the Holy Spirit has two primary goals:

1. *7God did not give us a spirit that makes us afraid but a spirit of power and love and self-control.* **2 Timothy 1:7 (NCV)** The power of God prepares, heals and equips the person who is experiencing the power. Even if that person only observes the power of God at work in others, that experience will have an impact. In other words, even seeing others experience miracles will impact your life by increasing your faith and trust in the Lord. Seeing others accept his power will help you receive his power in your life.

2. The power of God enables witnessing to others. The person becomes a stronger witness to the work of God because it is no longer just theological, but is practical and applicable to

life. Experiencing the power of God increases passion and devotion. The personal fire spreads to others.

QUALIFICATIONS:

Many people do not believe that they are qualified to either minister or receive the power of God for many reasons:

1. They think that they are too weak and do not have enough faith to work with or experience the power of God in their lives. Paul had to address this type of thinking for himself. He asked the Lord about it and the Lord said: *⁹But he said to me, "My grace is enough for you. When you are weak, my power is made perfect in you." So I am very happy to brag about my weaknesses. Then Christ's power can live in me.* **2 Corinthians 12:9 (NCV)**

   • What this means is that the power is God's power and has nothing to do with the minister or the character of the person who wants to experience God's power. It is for this reason that lost people can experience God's power and become saved because of it.

   • Recognition of your weakness helps you to remember that it is God who has the power. Your weakness keeps you humble and able to receive his power because you trust God.

2. They believe that God does not care enough or love them enough to use his power to change their lives.

3. They do not understand God's grace. Grace is "unmerited favor." Grace is given to us not because we deserve it or are qualified to receive it, but because it is God's will to touch us with his mighty hand.

4. They believe that only exceptional, talented people can either minister in or receive God's power. Scripture says: *¹⁰The Spirit gives to another person the power to do miracles, to another the ability to prophesy.* **1 Corinthians 12:10 (NCV).** This Scripture means that all born-again Christians baptized in the Holy Spirit, can minister miraculous power to others or receive that power in their lives. No special status is required for the Holy Spirit to give power to Christians.

Jerome A. Jochem M.S., M.A.

CONCLUSION:

Scripture tells us that we are to [34] *Announce that God is powerful.".*
Psalms 68:34 (NCV)

To announce that God is powerful we need to be able to experience his power in our lives. That means accepting God's power without fear or a lack of trust in him. We must stir up the fire of our passion, ignite the fuse of God-centered worship, and accept the explosive power of God as he anoints us through the Holy Spirit. Receiving the power is not just about us, the more we abide in his power, the more we can honestly *"announce that God is powerful"* to the world.

NOTES:

6

GOD'S TOUCH - ALLOW

Text: *¹⁴He will bring glory to me by taking from what is mine and making it known to you. ¹⁵All that belongs to the Father is mine. That is why I said the Spirit will take from what is mine and make it known to you.* **John 16:14-15 (NIV)**

INTRODUCTION:

Today I am preaching the final sermon out of a series of three. In the first sermon, I preached about abiding in Christ through God-centered worship. In the second sermon, I preached about accepting the power of the Holy Spirit. In this sermon, I will preach about allowing the Holy Spirit to touch your body, mind, and spirit to give to you what Christ wants you to have. Remember that God will never "take you over" to produce a response to his touch. He will not violate your free will, and so it is up to you to allow him to touch you with the power of the Holy Spirit. Jesus will give to you in the same manner that his Father gave to him. The Holy Spirit will provide you with gifts to bring glory to Jesus. There are several ways of looking at God's touch, and in each way, you can experience the glory of Christ:

PHYSICAL TOUCH:

When the anointing of the Holy Spirit is powerful, many people will react physically.

- For example, some will fall to the ground, some will feel paralyzed in their seats, some will shake, and some will either laugh or cry.
- These physical reactions are secondary responses to the power of God because they are not God's primary purpose.

Jerome A. Jochem M.S., M.A.

- When God touches a person for healing, some of these secondary effects will happen in conjunction with the healing. In other words, a person with back pain may fall to the floor and then get up with the pain gone.
- The problem with secondary effects is that they can be distracting and a bit frightening because the person feels that he is out of control of his body. The result is that the person may reject the blessing because of the physical secondary effects that he is experiencing.

PSYCHOLOGICAL TOUCH:
Many people need a touch from God to clear up mental and emotional conditions.
- God's psychological touch may stir up strong emotions so that the person can have an emotional breakthrough.
- God's psychological touch may bring back memories that need healing through forgiveness and reconciliation.
- God's psychological touch may instill such mental and emotional states as peace and contentment.
- God's psychological touch may reduce mental stress by providing reassurance and immediate counseling.

SPIRITUAL TOUCH:
God's touch can also have an enormous impact on a person's spirit.
- The Holy Spirit can initiate a deliverance session and free the person from bondage to evil or demonic spirits.
- The Holy Spirit can increase the sensitivity of a person's spirit to God's presence and glory.
- When touched by God, a non-believer can find faith and his spirit can be made new as the "new creation."

Under the influence of God's touch, the person can have very wide-ranging and intense spiritual experiences such as visions. With God's touch, there can be a deeper appreciation of his divine love, mercy, and compassion.

CONCLUSION:
The Word of God feeds our spirit. The Word also engages our intelligence and emotions. But it is equally valid that we need the

loving touch of our God not only to reassure us of the Word but also to relate to us as individuals and as a community. We are blessed when we have the Word and the Spirit together in our lives and our church.

NOTES:

7
GOD'S PROMISES

Text: *¹³When God made his promise to Abraham since there was no one greater for him to swear by, he swore by himself, ¹⁴saying, "I will surely bless you and give you many descendants." ¹⁵And so after waiting patiently, Abraham received what was promised. ¹⁶Men swear by someone greater than themselves, and the oath confirms what is said and puts an end to all argument. ¹⁷Because God wanted to make the unchanging nature of his purpose very clear to the heirs of what was promised, he confirmed it with an oath.* **Hebrews 6:13-17 (NIV)**

INTRODUCTION:

In the world, the most common belief about promises is that "promises are made to be broken." Breaking promises is particularly true in the realm of politics. Politicians tend to say what they think pleases their voters and then entirely ignore them after they are elected. Any promises made to the electorate are broken in the light of self-promoting political conformity.

Broken promises hurt people and can cripple society. We base our faith on God's promises found in both the Old and the New Testaments. God knew, because of our human experience with breaking promises, that we needed assurance that he would not break his promises to us. It is for this reason that we must understand the nature of God's promises, and how to activate them in our lives.

GOD'S PROMISES ARE TRUSTWORTHY:

God's promises transcend any human promises by magnitudes of greatness. Entire books exist about God's magnificent promises, but the question that remains is whether they are trustworthy? Can we depend on God to make them real? The following characteristics of God answer that question:

HE IS ABLE:

Humans break promises because they cannot fulfill them. A human being can commit only to find that he is impotent to bring that promise into reality because he does not have the knowledge, power, and authority to make the commitment real.

- God, however, is omnipotent and that means that there is nothing impossible for him to accomplish.
- Since he has the ultimate power and authority at his command, there is no promise too difficult for him to accomplish.
- God, therefore, has the ultimate ability to fulfill any promise that he has made either in the Old Testament or the New Testament.

HE DOES NOT LIE OR DECEIVE:

An intrinsic part of God's character is his holiness.

- There is no room in God's personality to either lie or deceive.
- In the human court system when a witness takes an oath, he says that he will "tell the truth, the whole truth, and nothing but the truth." To violate that oath is punishable by criminal law. Since God is the highest authority, not the law but his holiness confirms his pledge.
- Because God is holy, what God says he will do he does, and he will carry out any promise that he has made because to fail to carry out those obligations would make him less than a holy God.

HIS OATH CONFIRMS HIS PROMISES:

Three times in the old and the New Testament God confirmed a promise by giving an oath. (Genesis 22:16). His promises and his pledge are unchangeable and fixed so that we can place 100% confidence and trust in them.

- His oath reassures us that his promises are immutable.
- His oath reassures us that his promises are valid.
- His oath reassures us that his promises are sincere.

HIS PROMISES ARE CONDITIONAL:

God attaches conditions to enable the fulfillment of his promise.

- Attaching conditions means that each person has a role to play in the realization of God's promise in his life. For example, upon the condition that the person accepts Jesus Christ as his Lord and Savior then the promised salvation takes place.
- If the person fails to meet the condition, then the promise cannot be fulfilled, but this is not due to God's hesitancy or inability, but it is due to the person not meeting the condition.
- God's conditional promises place an expectation upon humanity both in the New Testament and the Old Testament. The expectation is the primary process by which God brings about his promises.
- It is critically important to realize and to see the fulfillment of God's promise; a person must be patient. (Vs. 15)
- The requirement of a condition upon a promise may give the appearance and feeling that our faith is being tested. Our faith is made stronger by such tests.

CONCLUSION:

Has God made an unfulfilled promise to you? If so, then you must adopt a position of obedience and patience. Since God is not a liar and can do anything he desires to do, your promise will come true to the glory of God.

NOTES:

NEVER ALONE
AGAIN - PART 1

Text: *²³I will be in them and you will be in me so that they will be completely one. Then the world will know that you sent me and that you loved them just as much as you loved me.* **John 17:23 (NCV)**

²⁶This message is the secret that was hidden from everyone since the beginning of time, but now it is made known to God's holy people. ²⁷God decided to let his people know this rich and glorious secret which he has for all people. This secret is Christ himself, who is in you. He is our only hope for glory. **Colossians 1:26-27 (NCV)**

INTRODUCTION:
Both these Scriptures declare and promise that Christ is in you. In this sermon, I am going to analyze and describe what it means to have Christ in you. These Scriptures are talking about a relationship between you and Christ, and so we need to discuss both parties of this relationship.

YOU WITHOUT CHRIST:
- The mind of every human being is in solitary confinement.
- The mind of each person exists within the brain, and there is no direct sharing of reality among people.
- Yes, we try to communicate and share ourselves through the five senses, but mainly by speech, yet we never fully experience the other person, nor have they fully experienced who we are because they cannot break through the barrier that is the confinement of our minds.

- In other words, you and I are alone in the world and must confront the world on our own.
- Everyone, without Christ, endures this imprisonment of the soul, and without Christ, there is no solution to the problem of our loneliness.

CHRIST IN YOU:

17the Spirit of truth. The world cannot accept him because it does not see him or know him. But you know him because he lives with you and he will be in you. **John 14:17 (NCV)**

A bridge is something that provides a link, connection, or means of coming together.

- The Holy Spirit is a bridge between your imprisoned mind and heart and the mind and heart of Jesus.
- Once this link is made firm at the time of salvation, you are joined to Jesus.
- Since you are now together with Christ, he is literally in you, and you are in him.
- This union means that you are no longer alone because Christ through the Holy Spirit has done what no human being can do, he lives in you and shares his personhood with you.
- The ultimate effect of this coming together with Christ is that you can now deal with everything the world can throw against you with the help of Christ, who has overcome the world and now lives in your mind and heart.
- Because Christ is in you, you become a victor in every situation, and there is only one condition. *9I loved you as the Father loved me. Now remain in my love. 10I have obeyed my Father's commands, and I remain in his love. In the same way, if you obey my commands, you will remain in my love.* **John 15:9-10 (NCV)**

THE ESSENCE OF OUR UNITY:

Our bond with Jesus is nothing less astonishing than his love. His love for us is the same as his Father's love for him. We are no longer alone because we experience and live in the love of God for Jesus through the Holy Spirit. To remain in that love, we must follow the commands of Jesus. Those commands are:

[37]Jesus answered,"'Love the Lord your God with all your heart, all your soul, and all your mind.' [38]This is the first and most important command. [39]And the second command is like the first: 'Love your neighbor as you love yourself.
Matthew 22:37-38 (NCV)

- The compelling truth about how to abide in Christ is to love. To remain in the love of Jesus, we must love him and others. His only command is for us to love in order to be loved.
- He promised us that if we love, then he shall never abandon us to our mental and emotional prison again. He will never leave us or forsake us. (Deuteronomy 31:6)
- The reality is that if we love we shall never be alone. We will always have Jesus within us, and his love will flow out of us to others.

CONCLUSION:

Because we have this connection of love with Christ, we are not alone in the world and anything we may have to deal with, we can do through Christ. Living in him and his life in us means that we have hope, joy, strength, and victory in life.

NOTES:

9
NEVER ALONE
AGAIN - PART 2

Text: *²³I will be in them and you will be in me so that they will be completely one. Then the world will know that you sent me and that you loved them just as much as you loved me.* **John 17:23 (NCV)**

²⁶This message is the secret that was hidden from everyone since the beginning of time, but now it is made known to God's holy people. ²⁷God decided to let his people know this rich and glorious secret which he has for all people. This secret is Christ himself, who is in you. He is our only hope for glory. **Colossians 1:26-27 (NCV)**

INTRODUCTION:
Both these Scriptures declare and promise that Christ is in you. In this sermon, I want to focus on what it means to have Christ "in" you by asking where "in" you does Christ abide. I will also show you how you can deepen your relationship with Christ in you, by using the tools that he has given you to increase your passion and knowledge of him.

WHERE IS HE?
When we ask a child to accept Jesus, we tell the child to ask Jesus into his heart. But where is that? To understand where Christ abides in all those who believe in him, we must look at the human mind consisting of memory, emotion, mental abilities, and personality. We are in contact with the universe in three ways:

1. The Now: The present or "now" is the only means that we are indeed in touch with the world. Reality consists of what is happening now.
2. The Past: The past is not real, but consists of memories of the now. Attached to those memories are the emotions we experience in the now.
3. The Future: The future is also not real, but consists of our anticipations and expectations of what will happen to us. We can project a future based on the past and present.

A significant bit of wisdom is that Jesus relates to us in the now.
- We can remember him in the past, but that is just memories of him.
- We can anticipate a relationship with him in the future, but it has not happened yet.
- If we want to deepen our relationship with Christ, we can only do so by focusing our minds and hearts on the present. It is in the now that we can fulfill our love for him and experience his love for us.
- Anything that distracts us from living in the present will also distract us from our relationship with him.

DISTRACTIONS:

The Past. What has been can seriously distract us from what is in two ways.
- If our mind is pre-occupied by the "good old days," then we diminish our contact with Jesus in the present. Past distractions can become so bad that the person lives more in the past than the present.
- By far, the past events which dominate the mind are most commonly those involved with sad and painful experiences such as bitterness, hatred, resentment, anger, depression, and sorrow. Dwelling on these past events can seriously interfere with our relationship with Christ in the present. In fact, they can block and diminish our conscious contact with Jesus.

The Future. What may be can also distract us from what is and diminish our relationship with Christ.

- The past lays a foundation for the future. Trials and troubles of the past may cause us to anticipate the same in the future.
- The Devil wants to make sure that we see the future with fear and anxiety. He will paint a picture of our future, which is desolate and horrendous. The Devil wants us to fear, and so those pre-occupied by the future may live with worry and anxiety, all of which distracts from our relationship with Christ in the present.

Given that the past and future can have such adverse effects, the questions we must ask are:

- How do we learn to dwell in the present so that we can be perpetually conscious of Christ?
- How do we decrease the influence of the past and the future so that we can focus on the present with him?

THE TOOLS:

God has not left us without hope. He has given us three essential tools to use that will help us stay in the present and abide with him. Each tool is designed to resolve the negative influences of the past, present, and future:

THE PAST:

[14] Yes, if you forgive others for their sins, your Father in heaven will also forgive you for your sins. [15] But if you don't forgive others, your Father in heaven will not forgive your sins. **Matthew 6:14-15 (NCV)**

The primary tool God has given to us to settle down our past so we can concentrate on our relationship with Jesus in the present is forgiveness. Forgiveness functions in two ways.

- It allows us to get through the hurts of past offenses, so they do not pre-occupy the present.
- It allows us to move beyond our sin so that it does not weigh heavily on us.

Both these effects allow us to attend to the present relationship with Jesus without distractions.

THE FUTURE:

¹²In Christ, we can come before God with freedom and without fear. We can do this through faith in Christ. **Ephesians 3:12 (NCV)**

The tool that God has given us to resolve and eliminate the fear of the future is faith.

- Faith and prayer, when combined, can bring both confidence and peace to our perspective of the future.
- When we are peaceful about our future because we have faith (trust) in God, we can stay in the present with confidence that he will work out the best possible future for us

THE PRESENT:

God has given us more than one tool to deal with the present. *But the Spirit produces the fruit of love, joy, peace, patience, kindness, goodness, faithfulness, ²³gentleness, self-control.* **Galatians 5:22 (NCV)**

- You will note that these fruits are actions or behaviors.
- These actions bind us to the character of Jesus.
- We do these things in the present as we abide in Christ and experience a transformation into the likeness of Christ.

These fruits also give us protection against those things in both our past and possible future, which act as distractions from the present.

CONCLUSION

If we want to know and love Jesus, then we must stay in the present and protect ourselves from distractions either experienced in the past or projected into the future. When we focus on the present, we must act according to the character of Christ by allowing the fruit of the Spirit to mature in us. As we mature, our connection and identity with Christ become stronger. In other words, by living in the present relationship with Jesus, we become more like him.

NOTES:

10

NEVER ALONE
AGAIN - PART 3

Text: *²³I will be in them and you will be in me so that they will be completely one. Then the world will know that you sent me and that you loved them just as much as you loved me.* **John 17:23 (NCV)**

²⁶This message is the secret that was hidden from everyone since the beginning of time, but now it is made known to God's holy people. ²⁷God decided to let his people know this rich and glorious secret which he has for all people. This secret is Christ himself, who is in you. He is our only hope for glory. **Colossians 1:26-27 (NCV)**

INTRODUCTION:
Both these Scriptures declare and promise that Christ is in you. We discussed in the previous two sermons the fact that Christ is in you only through your consciousness of the present. Christ is in you now! We also discovered that both anxieties about the future and memories of the past could distract you from the present where Christ abides. In this sermon, I would like to talk about the past as it influences your consciousness of Jesus because of memories of sin. The tool we used to keep the past from haunting us in the now is forgiveness.

THE POWER OF SIN:
All sin consists of rebellion against God or his Word. So, sin is an action that is evil. Evil is both progressive and transformative. The actions of Joseph's brothers illustrate the progressiveness of evil.

- They started with jealousy (Genesis 37:4), progressed to conspiracy (Gen 37:18), and ended with the intent to murder. (Genesis 37:20)
- Their sin advanced from jealousy to murder, and only the intervention of Reuben prevented Joseph's death at the hands of his brothers.

The condition of Joseph's brothers illustrates the transformative power of evil. The principle here is that sin can transform something good into the image of itself. There are two examples:

- First, the transformation we see in Joseph's brothers from protectors to murderers.
- Second, the transformation we see in Lucifer, from a high-ranking servant angel to Satan the profane.

All our sin includes these two characteristics. It gets more and more evil and transforms us into slaves as we become the embodiment of the curse of sin itself. *³⁴Jesus answered, "I tell you the truth, everyone who lives in sin is a slave to sin.* **John 8:34 (NCV)**

THE SOLUTION TO SIN:
The sacrifice of the body and blood of Jesus overcame the power of sin.

⁶We know that our old life died with Christ on the cross so that our sinful selves would have no power over us and we would not be slaves to sin. ⁷Anyone who has died is made free from sin's control. **Romans 6:6 (NCV)**

²⁵God gave him as a way to forgive sin through faith in the blood of Jesus' death. **Romans 3:25 (NCV)**

- The death of Christ on the cross stopped the progression of evil in our lives, so we do not commit ever more evil actions. We are free from sin's control.
- The blood of Christ reverses the transformative power of evil, so the new creation is free of the nature of evil. We become free from the image of sin with all its desires and temptations.

When we accept Christ, our present state becomes free. Being forgiven results in the freedom to be aware of Christ in the present, and to fellowship with him in the now.

Jerome A. Jochem M.S., M.A.

FORGIVING OTHERS:

We can often be distracted from the now by memories and hurts from the past behavior of other people.

- Memories of hurts can torment us into a kind of slavery to the past.
- Past hurts can transform us into bitter and unfit servants who want to control others legalistically.
- Our relationship with Christ in the now can be diminished by anger and violence

HOW TO FORGIVE OTHERS:

¹⁴Yes, if you forgive others for their sins, your Father in heaven will also forgive you for your sins.¹⁵But if you don't forgive others, your Father in heaven will not forgive your sins. **Matthew 6:14-15 (NCV)**

¹⁹Then Joseph said to them, "Don't be afraid. Can I do what only God can do? ²⁰You meant to hurt me, but God turned your evil into good to save the lives of many people, which is being done. ²¹So don't be afraid. I will take care of you and your children." So Joseph comforted his brothers and spoke kind words to them. **Genesis 50:19-21 (NCV)**

Three steps to forgive someone who has hurt you:
1. Forgive them using an act of will. Pray Father, I forgive them in the name of Jesus.
2. Forgive them using a behavior. I will not seek revenge or return hurt for the offense.
3. Forgive them emotionally. I will not feel anger and bitterness towards the offender as I heal.

Note: trusting them again is another issue which can only be regained by their behavior over time.

CONCLUSION

If you have got nothing else out of this sermon, remember the idea that forgiveness equals freedom. To increase your relationship with Christ in the present, you must not dwell on the hurts and wounds of the past. You must first recognize and appropriate the work of Christ in your life so that you can be forgiven and freed from the captivity of sin in the present. Then you must forgive others, so you achieve freedom from their past offenses and wounding. Accepting your own forgiven state and giving others forgiveness will result in the freedom to stay with Christ in the present.

NOTES:

11

NEVER ALONE
AGAIN - PART 4

Text: *²²But the Spirit produces the fruit of love, joy, peace, patience, kindness, goodness, faithfulness.* **Galatians 5:22 (NCV)**

INTRODUCTION:

This is the final sermon in the "never alone" series. In the last several sermons we focused on the fact that Christ abides in the present – the now of your life. To have a relationship with him, you must concentrate on him moment by moment without allowing fear of the future or hurts of the past to distract you from him. He has given you three tools to help you concentrate on the present. To eliminate the fear and anxiety about the future, he has given you faith. Remember, that the faith that God gives is to eradicate the hurts and hang-ups of the past, He has given you forgiveness for yourself and others. You should also remember that forgiveness means freedom from the past. Today we will talk about the final tool which is the fruit of the Spirit.

THE FOUNDATION OF OUR RELATIONSHIP:

To know Christ is also to know his Father. Knowledge means more than just intellectual understanding, it implies a relationship, and that includes our emotions and actions towards Christ.

- The foundation of that relationship is illustrated in the fruit of the Spirit because the fruit expresses the personality and character of Christ and through Christ the fundamental nature of God the Father.

- What is of even more importance, the fruit tells us how to act towards Christ as we establish and strengthen our relationship with him.
- Today, I am going to preach about three of the nine aspects of the fruit and how these elements dictate our relationship to him.

LOVE:

[37]Jesus answered, Love the Lord your God with all your heart, all your soul, and all your mind. **Matthew 22:37 (NCV)**

This Scripture tells us that we must develop a comprehensive love for God. It is an imperative and a commandment.

- It involves a revelation of the hidden things of our hearts and souls. Those things that we usually keep back from sharing with others.
- It involves the establishment of transparency of self. The willingness to expose all that we feel and all that we think to the review of God.
- Folk who have been married for many years show us the best example of this type of comprehensive relationship. When death breaks that bond, it is one of the most painful experiences that we can suffer. Many never fully love out of fear of loss in the future.
- Christ wants us to have an even more profound love relationship with him. We are safe in giving ourselves without limit because his love for us will never end. His love lasts for eternity.

JOY:

[4]Be full of joy in the Lord always. I will say again, be full of joy. **Philippians 4:4 (NCV)**

"I am coming to you now. But I pray these things while I am still in the world so that these followers can have all of my joy in them. **John 17:13 (NCV)**

The fact of the matter is that Jesus was and is a joyful person, and if we are to have a deep relationship with him, then we must share his joy.

- Sharing his joy is hard for us because we have been taught to focus on the suffering savior instead of a joyful savior.
- We are commanded to be full of joy in the Lord. So that means we must allow ourselves to experience his joy and respond to him with joy.
- This joy is not a matter of circumstances, but of a sharing with Christ the joy of our salvation and relationship with him.
- Remember that the next time you see someone laughing in the Lord, that they are sharing the joy of the Lord and responding to his joy with rejoicing.

PEACE:

[27]Peace I leave with you; my peace I give to you. Not as the world gives do I give to you. Let not your hearts be troubled, neither let them be afraid. **John 13:27 (NCV)**

This Scripture tells us that we have peace when our hearts are not disturbed by our circumstances, and our hearts are not afraid of the future.

- Trust in Christ and peace are correlated. The greater the degree of trust we place in the Lord, the more peace we experience.
- That means that to take the peace Jesus has given to us; we must have faith in him. That is, we must have faith that he can deal with our troubles, and keep us safe in the future.
- Both our past and our future can be very destructive to our peace in the present. When we reach out for the Prince of Peace, we will find Jesus ready to act on our behalf.

FAITHFULNESS:

Many Scriptures confirm that Jesus was faithful to his Father and his calling. Regardless of rejection, stumbling blocks, and barriers, he did his Father's will and not his own. Doing the will of God, regardless of personal cost is the definition of being faithful.

- We must relate to our faithful Jesus by being loyal to him.
- Ultimately this means we must know the will of God and carry it out at all costs.

- We can start by being faithful in the small things. For example, Jesus is committed to attend church each Sunday to be with you. We can show him our faithfulness by being at church to be with him.
- Jesus is faithful to provide for us, and we can relate to his faithfulness by giving our tithe into his kingdom.
- Jesus is faithful to save the lost, we can relate to Jesus by faithfully speaking the Gospel and bringing the lost to the Holy Spirit.
- The bottom line is that we can deepen our relationship with Jesus by first recognizing his faithfulness and then practicing being faithful to his will in our lives.

CONCLUSION:

To have a real relationship with Christ means that we have found common ground with him. He has provided the fruit of the Spirit so that we can walk that common ground with him, and as a result, grow closer to him, step by step. The fruit of the Spirit is a tool dependent on actions. While salvation comes by faith alone, our relationship with Jesus comes by behaviors that imitate Christ, so that we become more like him each day.

NOTES:

12

CHRISTIAN MATURITY

Text: *¹¹And Christ gave gifts to people—he made some to be apostles, some to be prophets, some to go and tell the Good News, and some to have the work of caring for and teaching God's people. ¹²Christ gave those gifts to prepare God's holy people for the work of serving, to make the body of Christ stronger. ¹³This work must continue until we are all joined together in the same faith and in the same knowledge of the Son of God. We must become like a mature person, growing until we become like Christ and have his perfection. ¹⁴Then we will no longer be babies. We will not be tossed about like a ship that the waves carry one way and then another. We will not be influenced by every new teaching we hear from people who are trying to fool us. They make plans and try any kind of trick to fool people into following the wrong path.* **Ephesians 4:11-14 (NCV)**

INTRODUCTION:

I enjoy talking with a group of Christians. Although the conversation may start off with some mundane topic, it will soon turn to their faith in Jesus. Over the years, I have learned to listen to my fellow Christians and found that they divide into at least two groups, each having a different level of maturity. I call these two groups the "has done" and "is doing" Christians.

MATURITY:

At no time in any Scripture that I know of, are we told to stop growing or maturing in our faith!

- Our text for today tells us we are to grow in unity of faith and the knowledge of Jesus.
- The measure of that growth and maturity is the degree to which we become Christ-like.

- The fullness of Christ within us is the only measure that counts regarding our maturity.
- Growth implies a change from a "baby" to a mature Christian. Peter said: *2As newborn babies want milk, you should want the pure and simple teaching. By it, you can grow up and be saved.* **1 Peter 2:2 (NCV)** So, Peter made it very clear the Bible is one of the primary mechanism for growth.
- If the Bible is a primary mechanism for Christian growth, then we must insist on keeping it intact, rightly discerning it and making sure we are learning the "full Gospel."
- The more we reject portions of the Bible, the less growth will take place, and so Christians will remain immature and ignorant of the full Gospel.

THE "HAS DONE" GROUP:

Without a doubt, this group represents the majority of Christians and is the first stage of growth. You can identify this group by their topics of conversation.

- They focus mainly on the Gospels and specifically on the actions of Christ.
- They talk about the actions of Christ because they are beginning to realize that his works express his love for them.
- Topically they talk about such things as his birth, crucifixion, resurrection, and ascension as it applies personally to their lives.
- You will often hear them say something like "I am saved because Christ has died for me - or has shed his blood for me - or has paid the price for my sins."
- At this level of maturity, the Christian is learning the "elementary" or fundamental doctrines of the faith and is characterized by a growing need to know more about Christ.
- This stage of growth may take years and is extremely important, but it is not the final stage of maturity.

THE "IS DOING" GROUP.

The Bible urges us to take the next step in our growth once we have learned the elementary doctrines of our faith. *1So let us go on to grown-up teaching. Let us not go back over the beginning lessons we learned about Christ. We should not again start teaching about faith in God and about turning away from those acts that lead to death. ²We should not return to the teaching about baptisms, about laying on of hands, about the raising of the dead and eternal judgment. ³And we will go on to grown-up teaching if God allows.* **Hebrews 6:1-3 (NCV)**

- This group carries with it all the truths that it learned from the Gospels and adds to those truths what it is learning from the rest of the New Testament.
- These additional truths are not instead of the Gospels but are in addition to the teachings of the Gospels.
- The Charismatic revival that took place several decades ago consisted of many Christians in the "has done" group moving into the "is doing" group. It was then that the term "full Gospel" started.
- Topically they talk about such things as the Holy Spirit, the authority and power in the name of Jesus, the spiritual gifts, the power of prayer, the need for personal worship in Spirit and truth, the courage to witness with spiritual power, and they give testimonies concerning God's immediate intervention in their lives.
- You will often hear them say things like: "God is healing me - God spoke to me - God has a message for you - or I am overflowing with the Spirit of God."
- While the "has done" group focuses on the actions of Christ as a means of understanding his love, the "is doing" group sees the manifestations of the presence of Christ through the actions of the Holy Spirit as evidence of God's continuing love for them.
- This level of maturity still desires to know more about Christ, but through an intimate relationship with him as revealed by the Holy Spirit.

THE PROBLEM:
Sadly, and regrettably, these groups are often in conflict due to their lack of understanding of each other.

- The "has done" group does not understand what the "is doing group" is experiencing since those experiences cannot be directly found just in the Gospels. They will often condemn and reject the "is doing group" as being cultist or radical Christians.

- The "is doing group" will become very impatient with the "has done" group and will often demean them or reject them.
- Both groups will often apply derogatory terms to each other, forgetting the unity of faith so strongly encouraged in Ephesians.

THE CONCLUSION IS THE SOLUTION:

Each group must give the other group some grace.

- The people in each group are where they belong and cannot be forced into one group or the other.
- Growth and maturity demands change, so it is necessary to eliminate any church dogma or doctrine, which prevents growth
- Church leaders must encourage growth and maturity.
- If dogma or rejection of the full gospel handicaps church leaders, then people will not and cannot grow, and this maintains the conflict between both groups.
- An attitude promoting personal growth must be cultivated in all churches regardless of affiliation, and unity will happen.

NOTES:

13

WARFARE IN THE SPIRIT

Text: *¹⁴We know that the law is spiritual, but I am not spiritual since sin rules me as if I were its slave. ¹⁵I do not understand the things I do. I do not do what I want to do, and I do the things I hate. ¹⁶And if I do not want to do the hated things I do, that means I agree that the law is good. ¹⁷But I am not really the one who is doing these hated things; it is sin living in me that does them. ¹⁸Yes, I know that nothing good lives in me—I mean nothing good lives in the part of me that is earthly and sinful. I want to do the things that are good, but I do not do them. ¹⁹I do not do the good things I want to do, but I do the bad things I do not want to do. ²⁰So if I do things I do not want to do, then I am not the one doing them. It is sin living in me that does those things. ²¹So I have learned this rule: When I want to do good, evil is there with me. ²²In my mind, I am happy with God's law. ²³But I see another law working in my body, which makes war against the law that my mind accepts. That other law working in my body is the law of sin, and it makes me its prisoner. ²⁴What a miserable man I am! Who will save me from this body that brings me death? ²⁵I thank God for saving me through Jesus Christ our Lord! So in my mind I am a slave to God's law, but in my sinful self I am a slave to the law of sin.* **Romans 7:14-25 (NCV)**

INTRODUCTION:

There is some controversy about this Scripture.

- Some interpreters say that it applies to Paul's life before his salvation.
- Other interpreters say that Paul is a Christian writing to other Christians describing the Christian life.
- The spiritual war Paul is describing applies to the Christian and non-Christian alike.

- The only difference is that the non-Christian does not have the Lord to save him from death.

THE COMPLICATIONS:

This battle between the mind that wants to do good and that agrees with God's law, and the flesh or sinful self that is subject to the law of sin is complicated by God's deliverance at salvation.

- Some people experience deliverance from dominant forms of sin. Such sin can be a habit, hang-up or hurt which drives them to self-destruct. For example, they may swear like troopers, but get delivered from addiction.
- Others are delivered from what appears to be minor sins, but are not delivered from the evil habit, hang-up, or hurt producing sin. For example, they may no longer use God's name in vain but remain addicted.
- God seems to deliver the newly saved person from the law of sin in specific areas of their life, while the law of sin remains valid in other areas.
- It is as if God removes us from the battle in certain areas of our lives while keeping us amid warfare in other areas.

A PRISONER:

The law of sin is the flesh doing something sinful, regardless of the will of God for us to do otherwise. As the nature of all sin, it is rebellion.

- Rebellion produces captivity to evil. (Vs. 25)
- Captivity to sin changes us and produces spiritual and then physical death. (Vs. 23, 24)
- Doing evil changes us by reducing our resistance to evil. We become slaves who do what we are told to do without question or choice.
- Our spiritual man cannot grow because it is held rigid in the grasp of repeated sin. We cannot move beyond our prison cell.

THE LESSON:

If God did not deliver you from a destructive sin and captivity at salvation, it is because there is a profound spiritual lesson you must learn. Keep in mind that God does not want you to sin, nor does Jesus approve of your sin. He does want you to depend on him to overcome your sin.

- You will struggle with death bringing sin until you learn what you need to know to be free.
- An example is Israel wandering in the wasteland until a whole generation learned to trust and be obedient to God. They had to be free of their slave mentality and learn to be warriors.
- If you have been struggling with a repetitive sin in your life, make a list of all that you have learned about getting free of that sin and then realize that God is trying to teach you something else, and you have not discovered it yet.
- It may be repentance, forgiveness, love, or merely seeking him on a more personal and profound level.
- Once you have learned the lesson that he wants to teach, then he will free you from the besetting sin which is destroying your life.
- Give him your heart and listen to what he has to say to you. Ask for the strength to repent and realize the depth of his loving forgiveness, then repent and enter his kingdom.

CONCLUSION:

If you are struggling with a repetitive sin in your life and need deliverance, then you need to know what God is telling you. Ask him and then implement what he tells you to do.

NOTES:

14

CHRISTIAN FORGIVENESS

TExt *²¹ Then Peter came to Jesus and asked, "Lord, when my fellow believer sins against me, how many times must I forgive him? Should I forgive him as many as seven times? "²² Jesus answered, "I tell you, you must forgive him more than seven times. You must forgive him even if he does wrong to you seventy-seven times.* **Matthew 18:21-22 (NCV)**

INTRODUCTION:

The Bible makes it very clear that Jesus requires his church to be fruitful, and that is the precise reverse of what the Devil wants for the church. One weapon the Devil uses to paralyze the church and to make it dysfunctional is offense. When a fellow believer sins against you, it is offensive, and it impacts the entire church. Once you understand that offense is of the Devil, you have the knowledge required to overcome offense and prevent the Devil from paralyzing your church in a quagmire of hurt feelings. In this sermon, I'd like to outline some of the dynamics of offense and what's required to overcome it.

SINS AGAINST ME:

There are different ways in which a fellow believer can sin against you. We can outline them as follows:

- He can reject you. Often aggressively such as stealing from you, or passively such as ignoring you
- He can demean you. Either aggressively such as verbal hostility directed towards you, or passively, such as gossip, slander or spreading false accusations and rumors.

- He can disrespect you. Either aggressively such as rebellion, or passively, such as sabotaging your plans or standards.

Being offended is a response to an attack, and you know you are offended because your emotional reaction is that of anger and the desire to strike back at them.

THE KINDS OF OFFENSE:

It's important to be aware that there are different kinds of offense, and some are not as purposeful and directed at others. The types of offense are:

- Imaginary offense: Imaginary offense takes place when your fellow believer has no intention whatsoever of offending you or sinning against you, but you see his actions or behavior as an offense. This kind of offense strictly takes place within your own heart or mind and is usually due to a miscommunication or misinterpretation of what was said or done by the offender.
- Accidental offense: The fellow believer meant to be offensive, but not to aim the offense at you. These kinds of offenses usually come from comments made during conversation, attitudes, and biases toward specific groups of people.
- Purposeful offense: The fellow believer meant to sin against you purposely and with intent, and usually practiced his sinful behavior against you as a form of vengeance or retaliation. The purposeful offense is the most difficult to forgive.

WHAT NOT TO DO WITH THE OFFENSE:

Most of us go through a three-stage process when we have been offended by some sin against us done by a fellow believer. Unfortunately, we engage in this kind of reaction, even though it is ultimately unproductive and may result in sinning ourselves. These stages are:

- We nurse the offense. By nursing the offense, we elaborate it and intensify it emotionally so that it becomes much worse than what happened to us. We mentally review the details of the offense, allowing each aspect to become increasingly hurtful and painful.
- We rehearse the offense. What we begin to do is mentally rehearse our response to the offense taking pleasure

in inflicting harm on the perpetrator of the offense. We meditate on ways we can strike back and inflict the hurt that we are feeling upon them either passively or aggressively.

- We disperse the offense. We talk to other people so we can get them on "our side." The more people who agree with us, the more self-righteous we feel and the more forcefully we can strike back because we have others supporting us.

Regardless of the kind of offense, if we allow ourselves to nurse it, rehearse it, and disperse it, it will have a negative impact on the body of Christ. And even though we may feel that we were the ones wronged, in the end, we hurt others by becoming as offensive and sinful as the perpetrator. Christ, therefore, gave us a solution about how to deal with the offense when a fellow believer sins against us. He wants us to deal with that kind of situation in a healthy and productive manner, rather than allowing it to become a source of discord and division in the church.

THE PATTERN TO OVERCOME OFFENSE:

[15] *"If your fellow believer sins against you, go and tell him in private what he did wrong. If he listens to you, you have helped that person to be your brother or sister again.* [16] *But if he refuses to listen, go to him again and take one or two other people with you. 'Every case may be proved by two or three witnesses.'* [17] *If he refuses to listen to them, tell the church. If he refuses to listen to the church, then treat him like a person who does not believe in God or like a tax collector.* **Matthew 18:15-17 (NCV)**

Just as there is a three-stage pattern to cultivate offense due to sin, there is a three-stage healthy pattern to deal with the offense. The stages are as follows:

- Go to your brother or sister and tell them what offended you and how you feel they sinned against you. You might find that he or she had no intention whatsoever of sinning against you and had no idea that you are offended by what he said or did. Resolve the offense by having an adult discussion, and establish peace between you and your fellow believer.
- If the person who sinned against you will not listen, then you must take several other witnesses with you and discuss the situation again. The purpose of the witnesses is not to

Jerome A. Jochem M.S., M.A.

entrap you or the other person, but to bring clarity where there is misunderstanding or misrepresentation. At all costs, these witnesses must avoid prejudgment, and the facts of the conflict entirely understood.

- The last step in the process is to inform your pastor, who represents your church, about the situation and allow him to intervene to bring resolution. Such resolution may include church discipline and may also involve the entire body of Christ. The only other option left is to treat the offender as a nonbeliever because he is not following the scriptural pattern for resolving the conflict.

CONCLUSION:

Always remember that offense comes from wounds to the ego. We all have an ego, and it will be wounded merely by human interaction. No church is perfect, and offenses will take place regardless of the kinds of offense or the intent of the brother who sins against you. It is essential then, for us to realize that we will not respond in a way prompted by the Devil, but will follow the Holy Spirit to a peaceful resolution of the problem.

NOTES:

15

THE FOUR UPS OF WORSHIP

Text: *²³The time is coming when the true worshipers will worship the Father in spirit and truth, and that time is here already. You see, the Father too is actively seeking such people to worship him. ²⁴ God is spirit, and those who worship him must worship in spirit and truth."* **John 4:23-24 (NCV)**

INTRODUCTION:

There is a direct relationship between worship of the Lord and relationship with the Lord. Experiencing intense worship results in experiencing a passionate relationship. Weak worship results in an inadequate relationship. To increase your experience of the Lord, you must increase worship. Four ways to improve your experience of worship are as follows:

1. Pray up.
2. Sing up.
3. Look up.
4. Be up.

1). PRAY UP:

⁷Give all your worries to him, because he cares about you. **1 Peter 5:7 (NCV)**
Often, we come into the worship time very distracted by the world because of:

- Worries and fears.
- Relationship problems.
- Personal problems.
- Child problems.

- Financial problems.
- Health problems.

The best way to deal with all these inhibitors to worship is through prayer. Pray before you worship, casting your troubles upon him, trusting him to provide an answer for you. If you do not pray before worshipping, then your worship will be weak. If you do pray before worshipping your worship will be strong.

2). SING UP:

Once you have gotten past the inhibitors to worship it is time to sing. But singing is not the point of worship. The point of worship is to sing to the Lord.

Sometimes this can be difficult because:

- You are unfamiliar with the song and therefore must try to learn it.
- The melody is complicated, or the key is wrong.
- You are concerned about what others think about your ability to sing.
- The song does not speak to your heart.

Overcome these barriers by remembering that you are singing to your Savior, and you are expressing your heart's emotions to him. Such feelings include gratitude, love, appreciation, trust, and thankfulness to mention a few. Singing up means that you are only concerned with what you are communicating to the Lord.

3). LOOK UP:

Looking up is the process by which you fix your attention entirely on the Lord. You may sense him in different ways, but in each way, you know that he is paying attention to you.

- When you "look up," you are not allowing anything or anyone in the sanctuary to interrupt your communion with the Lord.
- You are looking up when you become utterly focused on what you are sharing with him, be it emotions, a word of knowledge, a word of wisdom, or merely a state of peace.
- Looking up involves being able to be free to concentrate on the Lord during worship.

4). BE UP:

Intense worship brings heaven down to earth, and earth up to heaven. When overcome by the anointing of the Holy Spirit, then you are facing a choice. To "be up" with the Spirit or to stay earthbound because:

- You are afraid to let go due to a lack of trust in the Lord.
- You are afraid of what others may think about you.
- You need to control instead of giving control to God.

Always remember that the Lord has your best interest in mind and will never harm you. Be up to letting go.

CONCLUSION:

I think most of us at our church want to experience intense worship and the outpouring of the anointing of the Holy Spirit. To achieve this, we must work at it in so far as we have to control and eliminate the barriers to worship within ourselves and our congregation. Unity among us is critically important, as is the love and support that we give each other. We must be free to worship, free to be with the Lord, and open to experience what he wants us to experience without inhibitions. So, let us praise the Lord and worship him with enthusiasm.

NOTES:

16

NOTHING CAN
SEPARATE US

Text: *[35] Can anything separate us from the love Christ has for us? Can troubles or problems or sufferings or hunger or nakedness or danger or violent death? [36] As it is written in the Scriptures: "For you we are in danger of death all the time. People think we are worth no more than sheep to be killed." Psalm 44:22 [37] But in all these things we have full victory through God who showed his love for us. [38] Yes, I am sure that neither death, nor life, nor angels, nor ruling spirits, nothing now, nothing in the future, no powers, [39] nothing above us, nothing below us, nor anything else in the whole world will ever be able to separate us from the love of God that is in Christ Jesus our Lord.* (**Romans 8:35-39 (NCV)**)

INTRODUCTION:

Separation from the ones we love is a very sad fact of human life. Separation is an event which keeps us from giving ourselves entirely to those dearest to us because we know that ultimately, we will suffer their loss.

- It usually begins with our grandparents; they tend to leave us first.
- We may lose a parent next, or perhaps a brother or sister.
- Our absolute best friend may move away and leave us behind.
- We may get married, but lose the love of our lives to divorce.
- We may fall in love only to have that love unrequited and rejected.
- We may have a baby that is stillborn or dies shortly after birth.

In addition to people, we can lose a job, a car, a house, and other material things. With each loss, it becomes more and more difficult to share the deepest parts of our hearts with anyone. We can't share if we don't trust them to remain with us, regardless of what we are experiencing either good or awful.

THE LIGHT OF HOPE FOR CHRISTIANS:

Amid this dismal forecast of our continual abandonment, comes this astonishing proclamation from Paul about the enduring love of God through Christ:

[38]Yes, I am sure that neither death, nor life, nor angels, nor ruling spirits, nothing now, nothing in the future, no powers, [39]nothing above us, nothing below us, nor anything else in the whole world will ever be able to separate us from the love of God that is in Christ Jesus our Lord. **Romans 8:35-39 (NCV)**

I am sure: Paul was like anyone else and had experienced losses in his life. Such losses must have had an impact on his life
- What convinced Paul about the eternity of God's love was his experiences with God as he walked through life.
- It was during his times of victory and joy, as well as his times of persecution and suffering that Paul concluded that separation from God's love is not possible because of Jesus Christ.
- It is the same with us! Our daily walk with God convinces us that we will not be abandoned or deserted by God, regardless of the trials in our lives.

Death: Paul is not saying that we shall not die. Paul endured many sufferings that brought him close to death.
- He is saying that what survives after death shall be loved by God.
- The Christian spirit after death will not be rejected or neglected by God.
- Instead, the spirit will be brought into an even more loving relationship with God then possible while alive.

Life: This amazing statement means that the purpose of life's trials, tribulations, sufferings is not to separate you from God because that is impossible. We must not assume that God is rejecting us.

- It does mean that those tough times in life are designed to draw you deeper into God's eternal love.
- If you fully realize this principle, it can shed new light on why you are suffering. It is the secret of the martyrs that identifying with the sufferings of Christ also opens the door to identifying with his love.

Angels: No matter how beautiful, awe-inspiring, and holy angels can appear, they are not in competition with God. Remember that the only angel who tried to replace God became Satan.

- They do not understand salvation.
- They do not have the authority to proclaim religion and if they do it is false.
- They do not have the authority to judge and if they do it is a false judgment.
- So, they cannot break your loving relationship with God by any of these things.

Ruling Spirits: The only kinds of ruling spirits on this earth are the demonic spirits which influence and possess the hearts of human leaders. Such spirits are still active today.

- We can see their actions in the world today through demonized groups and leaders.
- Their actions stand out as pleasing to the Devil in that they kill, steal and destroy with abandonment.
- Their hearts and minds are deceived and distorted by the spirits that rule them so that no act is too evil or too cruel to be ignored.
- In fact, the opposite is true. The more horrendous and inhuman the act the better they enjoy doing it.
- Even these sub-humans cannot separate a Christian from the love of God.
- They kill Christians because: [22] *people think we are worth no more than sheep to be killed.* **Psalms 44:22 (NCV)** The fact is that they only free the Christian spirit into the loving arms of Christ.

Nothing Now-In the Future: This is a beautiful promise of God's continuing love for us now and in the future. He will never abandon us or leave us orphans.

- It speaks about the eternal nature of God's love. The rule of loss does not apply, and so we can safely give ourselves to him without restriction or fear.
- It speaks of the unchanging love of God for us. Unlike human love, it does not fade away, and time does not change it at all.
- It speaks of the supreme value of God's love for us. Nothing will ever become more important, precious, or desirable than God's love as long as it exists for us to experience.

A Warning and Conclusion

The promise of God's inseparable love for you remains eternally valid as long as you are walking in the Spirit and not the flesh.

- The one thing that Paul did not say cannot separate us from the love of God is a sin.
- Sin can break fellowship with God.
- While sin breaks fellowship, God still loves us but we cannot or will not receive it because we are in rebellion.
- So, while God still loves us, we can become separated from that love and experience judgment for our sin.
- It is not so much that God stops loving us, but that we stop loving God.
- The solution is confession and repentance, and we return to the love of God fully and completely.

Notes:

17
HOW TO CHANGE
YOUR LIFE

Text: [22] *you were taught to leave your old self—to stop living the evil way you lived before. That old self becomes worse, because people are fooled by the evil things they want to do.* [23] *But you were taught to be made new in your hearts,* [24] *to become a new person. That new person is made to be like God—made to be truly good and holy.* **Ephesians 4:22-24 (NCV)**

INTRODUCTION:

Many of us live in quiet desperation because we experience obstacles that are difficult for us to eliminate. Change seems impossible, and we must endure the same old pains, hurts, and self-destructive behavior that we have repeatedly experienced in the past. But that is not God's way or God's will for us because he has enabled us to change our lives in awesome and wonderful ways. Those who know the Lord Jesus Christ can change because he has made us into a new creation in his image. Here are some principles which will help you understand how to change your life.

YOU ARE A NEW CREATION:

- You have a new song: [3] *He put a new song in my mouth, a song of praise to our God. Many people will see this and worship him. Then they will trust the LORD.* **Psalm 40:3 (NCV)**
- You have a new name: [17] *"Everyone who has ears should listen to what the Spirit says to the churches. "I will give some of the hidden manna to everyone who wins the victory. I will also give to each one who wins the victory a white stone with a new name written on it. No*

one knows this new name except the one who receives it. **Revelation 2:17 (NCV)**

- You have a new heart: [26] *Also, I will teach you to respect me completely, and I will put a new way of thinking inside you. I will take out the stubborn hearts of stone from your bodies, and I will give you obedient hearts of flesh.* **Ezekiel 36:26 (NCV)**
- You have a new life: [4] *When we were baptized, we were buried with Christ and shared his death. So, just as Christ was raised from the dead by the wonderful power of the Father, we also can live a new life.* **Romans 6:4 (NCV)**
- You have a new agreement with God: [25] *In the same way, after they ate, Jesus took the cup. He said, "This cup is the new agreement that is sealed with the blood of my death. When you drink this, do it to remember me. "* **1 Corinthians 11:25 (NCV)**

YOU MUST BELIEVE THAT YOU CAN CHANGE:

[23] *Jesus said to the father, "You said, 'If you can!' All things are possible for the one who believes. "* **Mark 9:23 (NCV)**

After repeated failures to change, you may come to think that you cannot change.

- You fall into a state of hopelessness and give up the idea that life can get better.
- Scripture has a different message. It tells you that you can change because you are a new creation.
- The new creation is no longer entrapped or enslaved by the factors which kept you from changing in the past.
- Ultimately, you must come to believe that you can give up the old life with all its evil patterns of failure and self-destroying habits.

EVEN THOUGH YOU ARE POWERLESS, YOU MUST BELIEVE THAT GOD HAS THE POWER:

[27] *Jesus answered, "God can do things that are not possible for people to do."* **Luke 18:27 (NCV)**

In the past when we have failed, we were trying to do things in our way.

- We quickly find out that our way doesn't work and that we are in fact powerless to change.
- That sense of being powerless is the first step in victory because we soon come to understand that while we are powerless, God has all the power we need.
- Ultimately, we must depend on the Holy Spirit to change us, and we must follow the direction he is leading us to obtain victory over powerlessness.

YOU MUST BELIEVE THAT GOD WANTS YOU TO CHANGE:

28 We know that in everything God works for the good of those who love him. They are the people he called, because that was his plan. 29 God knew them before he made the world, and he decided that they would be like his Son so that Jesus would be the firstborn of many brothers. 30 God planned for them to be like his Son; and those he planned to be like his Son, he also called; and those he called, he also made right with him; and those he made right, he also glorified. **Romans 8:28-30 (NCV)**

- After repeated failures, many people come to believe that even God has given up on them.
- The truth of the matter is that God wants a change that is positive, fruitful, and pleasing to him.
- He understands that you do not have the wisdom or knowledge to be able to change on your own, so he sends the Holy Spirit to change you.
- You cannot even imagine how much the Holy Spirit can change your life by changing you and directing you to his fruit such as love, joy, peace, etc.

YOU MUST EXPRESS YOUR FAITH IN ACTION:

5 In your lives you must think and act like Christ Jesus. **Philippians 2:5 (NCV)**

Having the faith to change must be accompanied by action. These actions are of two types, the first being positive and the second being negative.

1. Positive actions are new behaviors and feelings guided by the Holy Spirit, which shape you to become pleasing to God.

Sometimes, positive actions are called righteousness and holiness.

2. Negative actions involve giving up or surrendering up your old lifestyle with all its bad habits and destructive feelings and ideas. Negative actions are called confession and repentance.

Be aware that hoping, desiring, wishing for, or imagining change will not bring about change only actions will accomplish that.

YOU MUST STRIVE DAILY TO BE THE BEST YOU CAN BE:

22 The LORD'S love never ends; his mercies never stop. 23 They are new every morning; LORD, your loyalty is great. **Lamentations 3:22-23 (NCV)**

- The ability to change begins at salvation, but salvation is not just a one-time event.
- Scripture tells us that God's mercies are new every morning, which means we must get a daily supply of power, wisdom, and strength to change in ways that please him.
- In that sense, every Christian is on a voyage of change, becoming more like Jesus Christ as they apply both Biblical and Holy Spirit principles to their walk-through life.
- Being human beings, we will fail and fall, but God is always there to help us back up and to continue our voyage into his presence.

CONCLUSION:

When we realize that we can change and become more like God, more in the image of Jesus Christ, our heart is full of joy. Only God can remove the mountains that we face, can level the valleys that we must walk through, and open our eyes that we may see his purpose in our life. Change should be welcome when that change is in the hands of the Almighty God our Lord and Savior.

NOTES:

18

BE HOLY

Text: *So prepare your minds for service and have self-control. All your hope should be for the gift of grace that will be yours when Jesus Christ is shown to you. ¹⁴ Now that you are obedient children of God do not live as you did in the past. You did not understand, so you did the evil things you wanted. ¹⁵ But be holy in all you do, just as God, the One who called you, is holy. ¹⁶ It is written in the Scriptures: "You must be holy, because I am holy."*
1 Peter 1:13-16 (NCV)

INTRODUCTION:
Unless we have a good understanding of holiness, we will never really know if we please God with our faith and conduct. Holiness is a difficult concept to comprehend. We tend to confuse being holy with sinless perfection, a condition which is impossible for us as humankind. (1 John 1:8-10).

MEANING OF HOLY:
The word holy has several meanings in the Greek and Hebrew languages.
- A primary meaning is to be set apart or different than something.
- A secondary meaning is to be pure or sanctified.
- A third meaning is a reference to something that is "an awful thing," and is translated into modern English as "something unimaginably awesome."

When examining the meaning of holiness, it implies a judgment. Something is judged as being worthy of rejection while something else is judged as being worthy of acceptance and affiliation.

THE SCRIPTURAL IMPERATIVE:
[1]*Dear friends, we have these promises from God, so we should make ourselves pure—free from anything that makes body or soul unclean. We should try to become holy in the way we live because we respect God.* **2 Corinthians 7:1 (NCV)**

[7]*God called us to be holy and does not want us to live in sin.* **1 Thessalonians 4:7 (NCV)**

Both Scriptures command us to reject worldly ways. Ways especially that are sinful and destructive to our walk with Christ. We are, mainly, to be different than the world, holding different values and behaving in different ways.

BEING DIFFERENT:
Being different does not mean being holy. Being different is of little value if the difference is only superficial. Superficial variations such as:
- The kind of clothes that you wear or don't wear.
- How long you wear your hair.
- The use of make-up or wearing jewelry.

The person following these rituals, rules, and regulations is not automatically holy. Different, yes, holy, not necessarily so.

TRUE HOLINESS: ¶
[28]*You will teach me how to live a holy life. Being with you will fill me with joy.'* **Acts 2:28 (NCV)**

[30]*Because of God you are in Christ Jesus, who has become for us wisdom from God. In Christ we are put right with God, and have been made holy, and have been set free from sin.* **1 Corinthians 1:30 (NCV)**

It should not be a surprise that our holiness is imparted to us through Christ.
- Our holiness begins with our affiliation, acceptance, and faithfulness to Christ.

- Once we have accepted Christ, we become the children of God, and we are empowered to learn how to be different from the world in meaningful ways.
- The rejection of anything sinful in life certainly is a requirement for holiness. Scripture is very clear about that: *But there must be no sexual sin among you, or any kind of evil or greed. Those things are not right for God's holy people.* **Ephesians 5:3 (NCV)** *⁴ He wants each of you to learn to control your own body in a way that is holy and honorable.* **1 Thessalonians 4:4 (NCV)**

The kind of discipline prescribed by Scripture is not humanly possible, so we need the help of the Holy Spirit to enable us to live holy lives.

CULTURE:

In addition to our personal tendency to sin, the culture we live in contributes to our resistance to holiness because it is resistant to holiness. The culture we live in now is almost a perfect example of cultural opposition to holiness because of the emphasis on "inclusion" and "equality."

- The concept of inclusion means that we should include everybody in the activities of society.
- The concept of equality means that everyone is to be treated equally in the benefits of society.
- In contrast, the concept of holiness means that you do not include sinful activities and that you are not equally yoked to the unsaved.

Since the Christian idea of holiness is in direct conflict to the socialist concepts of inclusion and equality, Christianity is now under attack and pressure is being placed on Christians to sacrifice holiness for the politically correct societal imperative. Christians often are labeled as being bigots, and haters, who should be ashamed and should capitulate their faith. Scripture has something to say about that too: *³⁸ The people who live now are living in a sinful and evil time. If people are ashamed of me and my teaching, the Son of Man will be ashamed of them when he comes with his Father's glory and with the holy angels. "* **Mark 8:38 (NCV)**

CONCLUSION:

God will enable us to live holy lives. None of us are perfect, but with the help of the Holy Spirit and the love and support of our brothers and sisters in Christ, we can become more like Christ who is holy. We need to stand our ground when pressured to give up our faith and our hope and surrender to God all in our lives that would make us less like him. Scripture gives us the promises, reinforces the idea of our holiness through Christ, and encourages us to move on with him. So, let us not be ashamed of our faith or our desire to be holy and separated from sin.

NOTES:

19
BE ENCOURAGED

T**ext:** *¹³ But encourage each other every day while it is "today." Help each other so none of you will become hardened because sin has tricked you.* **Hebrews 3:13 (NCV)**

INTRODUCTION:
I think it would be fair to say that everyone has experienced discouragement. Sometimes discouragement is accompanied by despondency and depression which becomes so intense that people give up. Other times discouragement accompanied by fear and anxiety about the future, has a paralytic effect on people. One thing for sure, discouragement is the primary weapon that Satan uses against Christians in general, but particularly against Christians who are involved in a ministry. One of the primary reasons that only a very few pastors will retire as a pastor, while the majority leave the ministry totally, is because of discouragement. The text today tells us that we are to be encouraged. Not only encourage ourselves, but we are to encourage each other as often as we can. How do we do that? What does it take to be an encourager to people suffering from discouragement?

BIBLICAL EXAMPLES OF DISCOURAGEMENT:
- Hagar after being rejected by Abraham: *¹⁵ Later, when all the water was gone from the bag, Hagar put her son under a bush. ¹⁶ Then she went away a short distance and sat down. She thought, "My son will die, and I cannot watch this happen. "She sat there and began to cry.* **Genesis 21:15-16 (NCV)**
- Moses at his commissioning: *¹⁰ But Moses said to the LORD, "Please, Lord, I have never been a skilled speaker. Even now, after*

talking to you, I cannot speak well. I speak slowly and can't find the best words. *:13 But Moses said, "Please, Lord, send someone else. "* **Exodus 4:10, 13 (NCV)**

- Elijah after being threatened by Jezebel: *4 Then Elijah walked for a whole day into the desert. He sat down under a bush and asked to die. "I have had enough, LORD," he prayed. "Let me die. I am no better than my ancestors. "* **1 Kings 19:3-4 (NCV)**

COMMON ROOTS:

Each of these three cases has something in common. Hager, Moses, Elijah all suffered a disconnection from their faith in God. They had lost their courage to walk as God wanted them to, and as a result, rejected God's will in their lives at least temporarily. Based on their stories, the recovery of their courage, and their obedience to God, we can discuss three practical steps that each of us needs to take to remain encouraged.

THREE STEPS TO ENCOURAGEMENT:

1. Develop an encouraging faith: *7I have fought the good fight, I have finished the race, I have kept the faith.* **2 Timothy 4:7 (NIV)**

   - An encouraging faith is a persistent, enduring, and persevering faith.
   - During discouragement, one must make it an act of will to find something to encourage you. During the greatest darkness, there is a light, and it is a matter of encountering it, and that is all about faith.
   - Remember that discouragement is a disconnection from your faith. Your faith is still there, but you have lost the vision to finish the race and to keep your faith strong.
   - Self-examination will tell you if you have placed your faith in anyone or anything other than God, and if you have, you need to return to your true source of faith, and that is Jesus Christ.
   - Develop encouraging thoughts: *12Fight the good fight of faith, grabbing hold of the life that continues forever. You were called to have that life when you confessed the good confession before many witnesses* **1 Timothy 6:12 (NCV)**. Discouragement is

a weapon that Satan uses against us because it engages us in a battle of the mind.

- To win that battle you must fight using your faith in the promises of God, and of your knowledge of God's character and love for you.
- Holy Scripture is critical in winning this battle, and it's in the Scriptures that you should dwell until you are no longer discouraged.
- Just remember, that when you feel discouraged, Satan is attempting to control your thought life through self-pity or self-blame, and you need the help of the Holy Spirit to take control back from him and become encouraged.

2. Develop Encouraging Words: [11]*The right word spoken at the right time is as beautiful as gold apples in a silver bowl.* **Proverbs 25:11 (NCV)**
    - Your thoughts determine your words, but your words also define your thoughts.
    - When you are in a battle with discouragement, what you speak is what you hear and what you hear is what you believe.
    - If you speak words of encouragement, then you will begin to feel and be encouraged.
    - Similarly, if you speak words of encouragement to other people, they will begin to feel encouraged and will support you in your battle against discouragement.
    - Remember that discouragement is contagious, it can spread throughout the entire congregation promoting hopelessness and helplessness. Also remember, that encouragement is contagious and that a good word spoken at the right time can become a miraculous gift.

3. Develop Encouraging Actions: [12] *You have become weak, so make yourselves strong again.* [13] *Live in the right way so that you will be saved and your weakness will not cause you to be lost.* **Hebrews 12:12-13 (NCV)**
    - Thoughts and words in themselves are not enough to promote encouragement. You must act on your faith.

- Many times, an encouraging action is one that stands in opposition to the discouragement or the situation causing the discouragement. We often call this "stepping out in faith."
- One of the most critical actions you can take is to cry out to God about your discouragement and ask him for help for you to overcome the situation causing the discouragement.
- Remember that God wants to help you be encouraged so that you finish the race well and to his glory.

CONCLUSION:

Encouraging faith, thoughts, words, and actions produce a lifestyle of encouragement. And because encouragement is contagious, merely being encouraged is a ministry to others facing discouragement. Just as we are to comfort others with the comfort that we received from God, we are also to inspire others with the encouragement we received from him.

NOTES:

20

DEALING WITH CATASTROPHE

Text: *13But Moses answered, "Don't be afraid! Stand still and you will see the LORD save you today. You will never see these Egyptians again after today.14You only need to remain calm; the LORD will fight for you." 15Then the LORD said to Moses, "Why are you crying out to me? Command the Israelites to start moving.* **Exodus 14:13-15 (NCV)**

INTRODUCTION:

I think most of us would agree that life has a way of bringing us to the very edge of catastrophe. Our situation is such that we cannot turn back, and yet we hesitate to move forward. There are a couple of reasons why we are in this unfortunate position:

- We may have made decisions and choices which we cannot take back. In other words, we are committed to the course of action we chose for whatever reason good or bad. So, returning to the "good old days" is not an option.
- We may be fearful of what the future will bring. Stepping into an unknown future, potentially filled with danger is easier said than done.

This fearful position is precisely where the Israelites found themselves after God had delivered them from Egypt and brought them to the Red Sea. The Scripture for today tells us of the steps we need to take when we are on the brink of catastrophe.

FEAR NOT:

Moses directly addressed the fear of the Israelites about the situation they were facing. He recognized the fact that the people were feeling fear of the fierceness of the Egyptian wrath that was about to fall upon them.

- Many times, when we are facing a fearful situation, we want to deny it. We want to ignore it or hide from it or treat it as if it is not real.
- Very often the first step is to recognize that we are fearful, but that fear is not the solution to the problem and tends to make it worse.

DON'T PANIC:

If we allow fear to dominate, then we will panic. Panic involves making bad decisions about what we should do about the fear-producing situation. These kinds of panic reactions never solve the problem but make it worse.

- Moses told the people to stand still instead of panicking (like trying to run away from the Egyptians), and if they did not panic, they would see the Lord fight for them.
- Not allowing panic must involve controlling our reactions to our situation in such a manner that we do not become alarmed and make the situation worse

TRUST THE LORD:

The Israelites knew that the Egyptians certainly had mass murder in their hearts. The Egyptian army was a trained military force that would have no reservations about murdering all of the Israelites without a second thought.

- Given such a situation, it is counterintuitive to expect the Lord to take up the battle. And yet this is the only option that the Israelites had because they were not trained warriors, and ill-equipped to fight the Egyptian army.
- It was at this point that Moses directed the faith of the Israelites to trust God to fight the battle for them. He also reassured the Israelites that the Egyptian army would no longer be in existence after God finished fighting them.
- When we are in a situation that is catastrophic, we need help to overcome the enemy and to establish victory. It is at these times that God, and only God, can help us.

- It is imperative, then, that we trust in God to fight our battles because we cannot fight the battle ourselves.
- As long as we trust in God, we are neither helpless nor hopeless against an enemy no matter how powerful that enemy seems to be. After all, nothing is impossible with God.

DO OUR PART:

Even though the battle is the Lord's, the Lord required the Israelites to do their part. They were told to cross the Red Sea.

- God wants us to do our part to overcome the enemy, even though we are entirely dependent on him for victory.
- The implication of this is that God wants us to partner with him to defeat the catastrophe in our lives. This cooperation will help us identify the fact that God is the ultimate source of victory and that we can trust his guidance and direction during times of crisis.

CONCLUSION:

As we walk through life, we are going to confront situations which smack of catastrophe. We are not alone in facing the issues that are beyond our resolution. Instead, we can be still and with a confident trust in God, see victory.

NOTES:

21

FINDING JOY IN
TROUBLED TIMES

Text: *²My brothers and sisters, when you have many kinds of troubles, you should be full of joy, ³because you know that these troubles test your faith, and this will give you patience. ⁴Let your patience show itself perfectly in what you do. Then you will be perfect and complete and will have everything you need. ⁵But if any of you lacks wisdom, you should ask God for it. He is generous and enjoys giving to all people so that he will give you wisdom. ⁶But when you ask God, you must believe and not doubt. Anyone who doubts is like a wave in the sea, blown up and down by the wind. ⁸Such doubters are thinking two different things at the same time, and they cannot decide about anything they do. They should not think they will receive anything from the Lord.* **James 1:2-8 (NCV)**

INTRODUCTION:

At first glance, the words trouble and joy seem to be mutually contradictory. How in the world can you possibly be joyful when the world is full of troubles? The path to finding joy in troubles has a lot to do with attitude, doubt, and belief. In this sermon, I want to give you an outline of the path to joy even when you are experiencing a lot of troubled times.

TROUBLED TIMES:

Different Bible translations use different words in the first verse of our text. For example:

- The NCV uses the word "trouble."
- The KJV uses the word "temptation."
- The NIV uses the word "trials."

These words are all related. Trouble can be a trial of faith. Trials can not only be troublesome but can also bring about temptations to sin. Trouble times is best understood as testing of faith, regardless of the specific nature of the trouble.

OUR ATTITUDE DURING TESTING:

When we are going through troubled times, we can develop some horrible attitudes. For example:

- We can become angry at God and others. Anger makes the situation worse because it is a negative emotion that leads to other negative emotions such as bitterness and resentment.
- We can become depressed because we feel hopeless and helpless about the trouble. Depression not only increases the problem but also extends the duration of our suffering.
- We can try to withdraw from life by emotionally isolating ourselves from the trouble
- We can focus on the pain which increases its duration and leads to other bad attitudes.

ATTITUDES:

Our text tells us that the ultimate purpose of troubles, trials, and temptation is to refine and strengthen our faith.

- Jesus faced temptation for 40 days after being led by the Holy Spirit into the desert. (Luke 4:1). Note that the Holy Spirit led him to into temptation, but the Devil did the tempting, not God.
- If tempted, then we must understand that God provides a way out of the temptation, as he promised in Scripture. (1 Corinthians 10:13)
- One positive attitude when dealing with trials is to be patient. Patience is mental and emotional endurance.
- Another positive attitude is to be willing to learn what God is attempting to teach through the trial. Always remember that God wants the best for you and is building your faith and not destroying it.

- Once you have learned from the trouble or trial, then you are much better equipped to deal with life because your faith has been increased and expanded.

WISDOM:
One possible reason for troubles and trials is that you lack an understanding of the situation causing the suffering.

- Our text tells us that we should ask God for the wisdom we need to resolve the trial or trouble.
- Asking God for insight and knowledge is prayer.
- Tongues become a useful spiritual gift when you do not know how to pray about a trial or temptation.
- According to our text, God is very willing to give you the wisdom you need to resolve the problem or temptation. He provides this wisdom generously and comprehensively.
- Although you might be able to discern God's wisdom, the best source is the Bible.

DOUBT:
Doubt can take some different forms:

- Doubt can be disbelief: A reaction or feeling the exact opposite of belief in God. The person does not believe that God either exists or has the power to help him.
- Doubt can be distrust: The person may believe in God but does not think that God will come to his aid. God seems to be remote and distant. This distrust is the double-mindedness discussed in our text.

The result of doubting God is a lack of blessings. Such doubt acts as a barrier in that it blocks receiving the grace God wants to impart to the life of the doubter.

CONCLUSION:
We can experience a real sense of joy even during troubled times when we realize that these times allow us to grow in faith. Joy comes when we have been patiently waiting on God to act. Joy is our reward for enduring with faith. Joy happens when we have the wisdom to become victorious over the trial or temptation. So, let us turn to Jesus the next time we are in trouble or are being

tempted to give up and surrender to suffering. Finally, let us pray that God gives us such a strong faith that being double minded is impossible. The strength of our faith is the most important joy as we voyage through life.

Notes:

22

PEACE

Text: *³³ "I told you these things so that you can have peace in me. In this world you will have trouble, but be brave! I have defeated the world."* **John 16:33 (NCV)**

INTRODUCTION:
I think that we all would agree that we live in a troubled world. Our troubles are of all different kinds and often seem to build up to the size of a mountain. We get stuck in the valley of helplessness and hopelessness which is a dark place, indeed. The text for today tells us that we can find peace in Jesus, but how is that possible?

OUR SPIRITUAL ACTIONS:
To find the road to peace in Christ, we must take specific actions to shift from anxiety to God's peace. Scripture says: *⁶Do not worry about anything, but pray and ask God for everything you need, always giving thanks. ⁷And God's peace, which is so great we cannot understand it, will keep your hearts and minds in Christ Jesus.* **Philippians 4:6-7 (NCV)**

Our daily Christian disciplines are a vital part of finding peace. This Scripture says that we must:
- Take control of ourselves by rejecting worry rather than cultivating it mentally or emotionally.
- We must talk to Jesus about our situation and in the process of praying ask for what we need.
- We must always remember what Christ has already done for us and give him thanks.

If we do these things, God will give us peace. His peace is independent of our circumstance, so it transcends worry. God's peace will help us focus on Jesus both mentally and emotionally, and thus peace will be maintained.

THE FRUIT OF PEACE:

Peace is one of the Fruit of the Holy Spirit. Being a fruit means that it can become part of our character.

- We cannot only find peace but as we mature as Christians, we can live in peace. Scripture says [27] *"I leave you peace; my peace I give you. I do not give it to you as the world does. So don't let your hearts be troubled or afraid.* **John 14:27 (NCV)**
- Christ is eternal! The fact that he is eternal means that the peace he gives us is also eternal.
- The peace of Christ is not dependent on temporary situations as is the peace found in the world.
- Knowing that Christ will give us peace enables us to quiet our fears and anxieties.

A DEFEATED WORLD:

In our text for today, Jesus says that he has defeated the world. Since we tend to lose our peace because of worldly concerns, it is vital for us to realize that Jesus has overcome the world.

- Defeating the world does not mean that the world will no longer have an impact.
- Defeating the world means that we as believers now have the choice of allowing the world to steal our peace, or keeping our peace through Jesus.
- The whole world is defeated, and that means that nothing it can send against us can destroy our peace if we trust Jesus.
- Note, however, that Jesus warned us that the world sends trouble our way. His promise of peace is realistic and not based on false hope. When problems come, then peace will be found in Christ.

GOD'S WAY:

One of the reasons that we do not have peace is that we are trying to solve our problems our way and are failing miserably. Scripture tells us: [5] *Trust the LORD with all your heart, and don't depend on your own understanding.* [6] *Remember the LORD in all you do, and he will give you success. ⁷Don't depend on your own wisdom. Respect the LORD and refuse to do wrong.* **Proverbs 3:5-7 (NCV)**

- Our path to peace begins with trusting Jesus for peace.
- Such trust demands that we give up our solutions to the problem and find his answer.
- His answer will bring a final resolution to the problem, reducing our troubles, and ushering in his peace.
- Once we have his answer, we need to implement it effectively because his solution is best for everyone.

CONCLUSION:

Peace is desirable and often elusive. We find real peace in Christ. He gives us peace through the Holy Spirit and by helping us to deal with worldly problems. In Jesus, peace is found between God and man as well as between men. If our world has little peace, that means we need more of Jesus.

NOTES:

23

HEALING - A WORK OF FAITH

INTRODUCTION:

In every church, there are people with diseases such as cancer, and the body of Christ must deal with such sickness regularly. It is important to remember that:

- It is a policy of the Devil to make as many Christians sick as possible.
- It is a policy of the Devil to inflict as much death through disease as possible.

Science tends to support the intent of Satan because it often dismisses the possibility of healing through God. So, words spoken by doctors become curses. The truth is that the only word that counts is what God says and what is in the Bible. So, it pays for us to review what God says about healing.

WHO IS THE HEALER?

We tend to look at famous healing ministries and call the minister a healer. In Exodus 15:26 God said that He is our healer and there is none other.

"I am the LORD who heals you." **Exodus 15:26 (NCV)**

- The Scripture from Exodus is an "I am" statement which speaks of identity and basic personality.
- He was speaking to Israel, but today his identity and intent are the same.
- Today in the church, God remains *"I am the Lord who heals you."*

WHO CAN BE HEALED?

⁵So Jesus was not able to work any miracles there except to heal a few sick people by putting his hands on them. **Mark 6:5 (NCV)**

These few healings took place in the hometown of Jesus - Nazareth, where the people rejected him because he grew up among them. Their familiarity resulted in dishonoring him and therefore his Father.

Even in an openly hostile community, healings took place.
- Believers can be healed.
- Unbelievers can be healed.

Healing is a powerful manifestation of the character and sovereignty of God.

HEALING TAKES FAITH OF TWO TYPES:

1. Faith on the part of the person who is sick. At least enough faith to ask for a healing. Remember that you do not get what you want because you do not ask God. (James 4:2)
2. Faith on the part of the person praying for healing: *Then the disciples came to Jesus in private and asked, "Why couldn't we drive it out?" He replied, "Because you have so little faith. Truly I tell you, if you have faith as small as a mustard seed, you can say to this mountain, 'Move from here to there,' and it will move. Nothing will be impossible for you."* **Matthew 17:19-20 (NIV)**

Healing and preaching that the kingdom of God has come are associated. (Luke 10:9)
- The faith required by the Apostles was that the kingdom had arrived and that they had authority in it to heal.
- The kingdom of God is where the policies and laws of God are valid.
- It is a policy in God's kingdom that those made sick by the power of Satan shall be healed.
- Healing takes place through deliverance from the authority of Satan and reversal of disease through the power of God in the name of Jesus.

Jerome A. Jochem M.S., M.A.

HEALING IN THE CHURCH

²⁸In the church God has given a place first to apostles, second to prophets, and third to teachers. Then God has given a place to those who do miracles, those who have gifts of healing, those who can help others, those who are able to govern, and those who can speak in different languages **1 Corinthians 12:28 (NCV).**

- This Scripture implies that multiple gifts of healing are "deposited" in the church.
- It is the responsibility of members to withdraw gifts of healing for the benefit of others.
- This responsibility requires that each member has faith that the deposit is there - like money in the bank.
- Not so much of an individual ministry as a ministry of the church.

HEALING OF NATIONS

It is not only individuals who receive healings but also entire nations of people can be healed:

If my people, who are called by my name, will humble themselves and pray and seek my face and turn from their wicked ways, then I will hear from heaven, and I will forgive their sin and will heal their land. **2 Chronicles 7:14 (NIV)**

It gives one an entirely different perspective about our nation and its people to see their sin as a disease that needs healing. Sin not only causes disease (although not all disease results from personal sin) but disease can cause sin. Addiction is an excellent example of a disease-causing sin.

There are four ingredients necessary for the healing of nations;
1. Humility: Understanding that we cannot fix the problem through law or socialism. The deep heartfelt passion that our national healing will be by the hand of God.
2. Prayer: Persistently asking God for his intervention and not allowing national events to discourage us.

3. Seeking: We don't have to find God, but we do need to have a stronger face to face relationship with him.

4. Repentance: Turning away from our rejection of the Bible, of God, and the pollution of his church. Such contamination takes place when the church adopts the values and standards of the world.

CONCLUSION:

It takes faith in God to preach, teach, and accept healing in the church. Once believed, healing of all disease is possible, and the church can celebrate and rejoice in our loving and healing God. Be healed!

NOTES:

24

SHALL WE LOVE
EACH OTHER?

Text: *⁴Love is patient, love is kind. It does not envy, it does not boast, it is not proud. ⁵It is not rude, it is not self-seeking, it is not easily angered, it keeps no record of wrongs. ⁶Love does not delight in evil but rejoices with the truth. ⁷It always protects, always trusts, always hopes, always perseveres. ⁸Love never fails.* **1 Corinthians 13:4-8 (NCV)**

INTRODUCTION:

One of the most precise measures of Christian maturity is the ability to love. In today's Scripture, the word love (in the Greek it is called Agape) means "to be benevolent," and in some older translations, the word charity is used instead of love. It is important to note that we are not talking about emotion when it comes to agape, we are merely talking about how we act towards each other. So, we are encouraged to love through our behavior, not our emotions or desires. As a result, we can learn to love even if the feelings of love are not present. The question I would like to answer in this sermon is what do we have to learn to please God by loving each other as he desires us to do? Paul establishes two categories of loving actions. These include positive steps that we should do and negative actions that we should not do. I will discuss what we should not do first and then follow with the positive, loving actions.

NO ENVY OR BOASTING OR PRIDE:

Envy, boasting, and being prideful results from self-centeredness. When we envy we focus on what others have and what we do not have. When we boast we try to make others believe that we are more than what we are. Being prideful means that we esteem ourselves higher than other people.

- One way to defeat envy is to refuse to compare ourselves to other people. Our focus needs to be on our relationship with Christ, which is precious, rather than comparing ourselves to others.
- Prevent boasting by rejecting the idea that we must proclaim and emphasize what we have compared to what other people have. Very often boasting originates from envy as the person tries to compensate for his feelings of not being worthy or equal to other people.
- Pride is often a behavior which is a compensation for feelings of inadequacy and failure. Pride gives an individual a false concept of his value and is of the family of envy and boasting.

NO RUDENESS OR SELF-SEEKING:
A rude person is someone who tramples on other people's feelings without concern about the impact of what he is saying and doing.

A self-seeking person is someone who has only one concern and desire, and that is to get what he wants from others or to accomplish his personal goals despite the needs of others.

Both rudeness and self-seeking can be controlled by focusing on the other person's needs and developing sensitivity and self-control as to what is being said or done concerning that person.

NO QUICK ANGER OR GRUDGE HOLDING:
[24]Do not make friends with a hot-tempered man, do not associate with one easily angered, [25]or you may learn his ways and get yourself ensnared. **Proverbs 22:24-25 (NIV)**

Anger itself is not a sin, but what we do with that anger can be sinful. This Old Testament Scripture shows us why we should not be quick to become angry or hold a grudge or an offense against someone else because that ensnares us.

- Paul speaks about keeping a "record of wrongs." It's this action of keeping a record of grudges and offenses that causes bondage to bitterness and anger.
- The only solution to this state of bondage is forgiveness through love.

NO DELIGHTING IN EVIL, BUT REJOICES WITH TRUTH:
⁸Most importantly, love each other deeply, because love will cause many sins to be forgiven. **1 Peter 4:8 (NCV)**

In this verse, Peter is also using the Greek word "Agape" for love. What Peter is saying is that we are to go out of our way if need be to be benevolent and charitable to other people.
- Such deep love may be at a cost to us, but even so, we will rejoice with the truth that love gives us.
- In Peter's statement, love will cause us to forgive many sins committed against us.
- Note, however, that Peter did not say in the Scripture that love justifies any sin whatsoever. Modern day culture has gotten confused in that love is promoted as an excuse to sin. This idea is a twisted and distorted interpretation of Scripture and the function of love in Christianity.

IS PATIENT AND KIND:
Paul begins his discussion about love with positive behaviors. We are to be patient and kind to each other.
- Older translations use the term long-suffering instead of patient. That older term is more descriptive in that it implies that we are to tolerate each other even when we are being irritated by the other person.
- Being patient is godly because God is very patient with us. He gives us the benefit of the doubt and continues to have a relationship with us even when we are less than worthy of such a relationship.
- Being kind is also a behavior. It begins with the choice as to how we will respond to others.

- Being kind means, we will choose not to react aggressively or hostilely towards someone else, even if that person has offended us.
- Being patient and kind benefits us emotionally because we do not have to deal with the stress that results if we fail to make the right choice in these areas.

ALWAYS PROTECTS AND TRUSTS:

Some of the older translations use the word "to bear" instead of the word protect.

- The use of the phrase "to bear," implies that instead of being critical of other people, a loving person covers that person with silence. In other words, it's an act of love according to Paul to remain silent instead of being critical of and rejecting another person. In this manner, the person remains clear of gossip and false accusations.
- The word trust means merely to have faith. It is an act of love to place your faith in another person because it encourages that person to be the best he can. That same love covers a wealth of character defects because nobody is perfect

ALWAYS HOPES AND PERSEVERES:

To hope in the sense of this Scripture is to believe the best possible future for yourself and other people. Of course, our greatest hope is in the Lord Jesus Christ. But it is apparently an act of love to hope for the best for others in the church.

- Hope is not enough if there is no perseverance when things look the worst. That is the time for the greatest hope and for the most exceptional determination to love regardless of the circumstances.
- Hope and perseverance allow love to prevail.

NEVER FAILS:

Simply put love can stumble and fall, but it never fails.

- Love may die, but it also can be resurrected.
- Love seems to be weak, but it is the most potent force for all of humanity.

Jerome A. Jochem M.S., M.A.

CONCLUSION:

The most significant asset a church can have is love. Without love, it is not possible to please God no matter how big the church, how wealthy the church, how talented the church, or how entertaining the church. But love needs to be practiced among members because an effort needs to be made to love each other truly. The answer to the question shall we love each other should be an enthusiastic yes.

NOTES:

25

THE LION'S FOOD

Text: *⁸Control yourselves and be careful! The devil, your enemy, goes around like a roaring lion looking for someone to eat.* **1 Peter 5:8** (**NCV**)

¹⁸ "So listen to the meaning of that story about the farmer. ¹⁹What is the seed that fell by the road? That seed is like the person who hears the message about the kingdom but does not understand it. The Evil One comes and takes away what was planted in that person's heart. ²⁰And what is the seed that fell on rocky ground? That seed is like the person who hears the teaching and quickly accepts it with joy. ²¹But he does not let the teaching go deep into his life, so he keeps it only a short time. When trouble or persecution comes because of the teaching he accepted, he quickly gives up. ²²And what is the seed that fell among the thorny weeds? That seed is like the person who hears the teaching but lets worries about this life and the temptation of wealth stop that teaching from growing. So the teaching does not produce fruit in that person's life.²³But what is the seed that fell on the good ground? That seed is like the person who hears the teaching and understands it. That person grows and produces fruit, sometimes a hundred times more, sometimes sixty times more, and sometimes thirty times more." **Matthew 13:18-23** (**NCV**)

INTRODUCTION:

If you belong to a church for any length of time, you will confront a puzzling and somewhat sad set of facts about people in the church. I am talking about people who you thought were strong Christians, full of love for the church and the Lord, and mature in their walk, but they have left their walk with the Lord, are engaged in a lot of worldly activity, and seem to be proud that they are no longer walking in the Christian faith. Some would still claim to be Christian, but a review of their lifestyle would show that their Christianity is diluted and perhaps polluted by the values, attitudes, and desires of the world. The spiritual state of such people should sadden our hearts, but it also forces us to examine our church to see if it failed them in some way. So, the question that we should ask ourselves is why people who were apparently passionate about the Lord Jesus Christ and Christianity eventually leave both and then embed themselves in the world? Perhaps, an even more critical question is whether there is anything in you that would allow you to fall away from Christ and his church?

THE ENEMY:

The first text for today tells us that we all have an enemy who desires to consume our faith and strip us of our Christianity. This text shows us that this enemy, called the lion, is Satan, and it also implies that the Devil is aggressively attacking your faith through temptation and worldly involvement.

There are a couple of things we need to keep in mind:
- The Devil can only tempt, he cannot force us to reject Christ or the church.
- The Devil can try to make you into a victim, but you have the authority and power to subdue and reject him and his works.

If the Devil cannot force us to reject Christ, and we have the power and authority to overcome the Devil, then there must be something internal to us which allows us to fall. To understand those internal factors, we need to turn to our text for today.
- In this Scripture portion, Christ was instructing his disciples about evangelism. Primarily, what he said was that only one out of every four persons who hear the gospel would be fruitful in their Christian walk and maintain their faith in Christ over time.
- While an evangelist wrote this Scripture, we can also see those internal factors in each person that resulted in either productivity or failure in their Christian life.
- So, we need to take a close look at the personal dynamics to understand how people remain faithful to Christ or eventually reject him.

THE LACK OF UNDERSTANDING:

The second text talks about people who cannot grasp the gospel message, and they cannot put it together with the everyday lives they lead. (Vs. 19)

- In other words, they compartmentalize the gospel as "religion" and keep it separate from their daily lives.
- Since they are not living their faith in Christ, that faith soon becomes devalued and eventually rejected.
- They may still identify themselves as Christians, but they are Christians in name only and not in values, attitudes, and life choices.
- These people are particularly subject to a worldview that is popular, commonly accepted by most people but is unbiblical.
- Very often these people are legalistic or ritualistic Christians who either become hurt by legalism in the church or grow tired of empty ritual. Either way, they choose to leave even though at one time they were passionate Christians who loved the church.

THE LACK OF SURRENDER:

I believe that the most significant of all the factors which cause people to leave the faith and the church is a lack of surrender to Christ. (Vs. 21)

- When we surrender to Christ, we must surrender everything to him whether it be good and bad, or happy and sad.
- Of most importance, we must surrender to Christ that which is of the greatest value to us.
- To hold something of yourself from Christ, or to keep something in reserve is to invite the enemy to destroy your walk with Christ.
- The New Testament story of Ananias and his wife Sapphira in the Book of Acts (Acts 5) illustrates what happens when you keep something back from the Lord. In the Book of Acts, the result was death.
- The death of your faith and your walk with Christ can also take place if you hold back part of yourself from the Lord by

refusing to surrender it to him. God wants all not just part of you.

- You keep something from the Lord so that you have something to fall back on if you feel the Lord has failed you or when you run into troubled times.
- Today, there are a lot of Christians in name only who are removing themselves from the faith because they fear persecution or because it is no longer profitable or acceptable to be a Bible-believing follower of Jesus Christ.

THE LACK OF LOVE:

The final group of people who will fall away is those who suffer from a lack of love for Jesus Christ as demonstrated by a lack of faith that he loves them. (Vs. 22)

- The realization of the degree to which God loves you grows as you trust him to deal with the problems in your life.
- The faith that you have that Christ is for you and not against you, that he will work on your behalf to deliver you from the stresses of the world, and that you can depend on him for your necessities, develops as you see him change your life to improve it.
- If you see, however, the stress, tensions, and problems of life as indicators that Christ does not love or care for you, then your faith will not grow.
- Remember, to have great faith you must have a profound realization of his great love for you.

CONCLUSION:

The lack of understanding about Christ, the lack of surrender of all that you are to Christ, and the lack of belief and trust in his great love for you may cause you to reject Christ and his church. Each person needs to examine themselves to determine if there is a lack in their Christian identity. If so, the solution is to throw yourself upon Christ, to ask him to show you the importance of your Christian walk, to help you surrender those hidden places, and to deepen your love for him. We may not be able to do this without him, but surely, we can do this with him.

NOTES:

26

DEALING WITH DOUBT

Text: *³¹Immediately Jesus reached out his hand and caught Peter. Jesus said, "Your faith is small. Why did you doubt?"* **Matthew 14:31 (NCV)**

INTRODUCTION:

What if I have doubts? Is doubting a sin? If you are honest with yourself, you will admit that you have doubts about the Christian faith. Such uncertainties may include:

- Is Jesus who he says he is?
- Is the Word true and without error?
- Does God love you and has he saved you?
- Is Jesus the only way to a relationship with God the Father?
- Will you live after death?

When you have these kinds of doubts, it is because you are dealing with an area in which your faith does not exist or has grown weak. In the face of doubt, you have three actions:

1. You can remain an unbeliever and deny yourself the benefits of salvation.
2. You can feel guilty and condemned. You will hide your doubts by suppressing them and by pretending they don't exist.
3. You can admit that you have these doubts and then take steps to resolve them permanently.

Doubt was resolved correctly in the following two case studies:

Case 1: John the Baptist Doubts:
The Doubt: *²John the Baptist was in prison, but he heard about what Christ was doing. So John sent some of his followers to Jesus. ³They asked him, "Are*

you the One who is to come, or should we wait for someone else?" **Matthew 11:2-3 (NCV)**

THE ANSWER OF JESUS

⁴Jesus answered them, "Go tell John what you hear and see: ⁵The blind can see, the crippled can walk, and people with skin diseases are healed. The deaf can hear, the dead are raised to life, and the Good News is preached to the poor.⁶Those who do not stumble in their faith because of me are blessed." **Matthew 11:4-6 (NCV)**

John the Baptist is the man who said,
- *"Look, the lamb of God."* **John 1:29 (NCV)**
- *²⁷He is the One who comes after me. I am not good enough to untie the strings of his sandals."* **John 1:27 (NCV)**
- *"This man is the Son of God."* **John 1:34b (NCV)**

But while suffering in prison and unsure of his fate, he asks: *"Are you the one?"* (Vs. 3)

Like John the Baptist, your doubt may be answered intellectually, while at other times it demands an emotional experience. That is why in resolving our doubt we must ask for answers or an encounter with God.

YOUR ANSWER:
- Some people feel that we should never question the reality of our beliefs, but the Word recognizes that doubts will come. Note: Jesus did not rebuke John for his doubts.
- Jesus answered John's doubt by providing real evidence. Jesus is not afraid of doubt, nor should we be afraid that he will reject us when we doubt.
- It is clear though that Jesus does not want us to live in doubt. Living in doubt will happen if we lack the courage to confront doubt and the faith to believe in his answer.

CASE 2: THOMAS DOUBTS:

The Doubt: *²⁴Thomas (called Didymus), who was one of the twelve, was not with them when Jesus came. ²⁵The other followers kept telling Thomas, "We saw the Lord." But Thomas said, "I will not believe it until I see the nail marks in his hands and put my finger where the nails were and put my hand into his side."* **John 20:24-25 (NCV)**

THE ANSWER OF JESUS:
[27]Then he said to Thomas, "Put your finger here, and look at my hands. Put your hand here in my side. Stop being an unbeliever and believe." [28]Thomas said to him, "My Lord and my God!" [29]Then Jesus told him, "You believe because you see me. Those who believe without seeing me will be truly happy." **John 20:27-29 (NCV**

- When Jesus was heading into danger in Jerusalem, it was Thomas who said: *Let us also go so that we can die with him."* **John 11:16 (NCV)**
- Thomas believed in the Lord Jesus to such an extent that he was willing to die for him rather than abandon him.
- Thomas refused to believe that Jesus was alive and risen and probably thought that some imposter had deceived the apostles.

YOUR ANSWER:
- Jesus addressed Thomas's doubt when Jesus allowed him to examine his wounds.
- Once again, we see Jesus providing real evidence to help Thomas. He wanted Thomas to become a believer rather than an unbeliever.
- Jesus did not reject Thomas because Thomas had doubts. Instead, Jesus made a special effort to help Thomas believe. Jesus will help us resolve our doubts **as**

WHAT TO DO:
Remember that doubt can be of two kinds:

1. Intellectual doubt usually concerns whether the Word is correct and valid. For example:
   - Did Christ resurrect from the dead?
   - Will I be resurrected as Christ was, even though I have not seen anyone return from the dead?
2. Emotional doubt is usually not spoken out loud. It is an emotional reaction to a circumstance which contradicts faith. For example:

- Fear of sickness or death.
- Depression about the future.
- Experiencing anxiety about provision.

YOUR SOLUTION TO DOUBT:

- Overcome intellectual doubt by studying and absorbing the Word. Understand that God is not a liar nor does he give false promises.
- Overcome emotional doubt by personal and direct contact with Jesus through the Holy Spirit.

CONCLUSION:

Our circumstances can weaken faith or belief. Doubt is a symptom of weak faith or no faith.

Jesus understands that our level of doubt and faith will vary. Jesus is willing to work with our weak faith to strengthen it by resolving our doubts. Doubt limits us regarding the blessings we can receive and give to others. The more doubt we have, the less we can bless. Remember that to resolve doubt we must face it, using the Word and our knowledge of God to confront our doubts. Don't try to suppress, hide from, or deny doubt – that only makes it worse and prolongs your suffering from a lack of faith.

NOTES:

27
THE PERSONAL MINISTRY OF THE HOLY SPIRIT

Text: *¹⁵"If you love me, you will obey my commands. ¹⁶I will ask the Father, and he will give you another Helper to be with you forever— ¹⁷the Spirit of truth. The world cannot accept him, because it does not see him or know him. But you know him, because he lives with you and he will be in you.* **John 14:15-17 (NCV)**

INTRODUCTION:

In many Spirit-filled churches, the Holy Spirit is recognized mainly regarding the spiritual gifts mentioned in 1 Corinthians chapter 12. While the spiritual gifts are essential for a dynamic and healthy church, the Holy Spirit also has ministries which are more personal both regarding his personality and of the needs of the person to which he is ministering.

In this sermon, I would like to discuss five aspects of his ministry that are important to you:
1. The Spirit of conviction.
2. The Spirit of righteousness.
3. The Spirit of counsel.
4. The Spirit of comfort.
5. The Spirit of truth.

THE SPIRIT OF CONVICTION:

⁸When the Helper comes, he will prove to the people of the world the truth about sin, about being right with God, and about judgment. **John 16:8 (NCV)**

The Holy Spirit brings conviction which is an intense emotional reaction of sorrow for sin and a great hunger and need for Christ and salvation.

- There is a significant difference between conviction and condemnation. (Romans 8:1)
- Conviction focuses on sinful behavior and brings about repentance.
- Condemnation focuses on the unworthiness of the person and brings no change in behavior.
- The difference between renewal and revival is determined by the presence or absence of the Spirit of conviction.

THE SPIRIT OF RIGHTEOUSNESS:

⁹He will prove to them that sin is not believing in me. ¹⁰He will prove to them that being right with God comes from my going to the Father and not being seen anymore. **John 16:9-10 (NCV)**

Righteousness means "right standing" with God. Jesus imparts that right standing with God as soon as we believe in him. Jesus quite literally stands before God and declares our righteousness because of his work on the cross.

- The Holy Spirit brings us a sense that we can and do stand before the very throne of God as we praise him and send him our prayers and petitions.
- There's a difference between righteousness and self-righteousness.
- Righteousness is imparted and learned through the guidance of the Holy Spirit.
- Self-righteousness is a proclamation based on our opinion of ourselves, rather than the work of Christ. God always judges self-righteousness.

THE SPIRIT OF COUNSEL:

Have you ever had a problem in your life would seem to you to be unsolvable? No matter how hard you tried, or how many solutions you've applied, the problem remains and is a matter of fact may be beyond your ability to either understand or solve.

- The Holy Spirit can become your counselor to help you solve that insolvable problem.
- You need to expect a Holy Spirit solution and not something that is mundane or even something that you can understand. For example, he may tell you to forgive someone for an atrocity done to you or your family.
- Receiving the counseling of the Holy Spirit is dependent on listening to his voice. We are often too busy laying down our petition to hear the solution.
- The solution may come through prophecy, by church leadership, or by the Holy Spirit directly.

THE SPIRIT OF COMFORT:

15 "If you love me, you will obey my commands. 16 I will ask the Father, and he will give you another Helper to be with you forever— 17 the Spirit of truth. The world cannot accept him, because it does not see him or know him. But you know him, because he lives with you and he will be in you. **John 14:15-17 (NCV)**

Helper is the same as "Counselor" or "Comforter." For an individual suffering from a loss or hurt, the Holy Spirit personally comes to bring comfort:

- He brings companionship in a time of loneliness.
- He brings compassion in a time of suffering.
- He brings reassurance in a time of uncertainty.
- He brings encouragement at a time of failure and discouragement.
- He speaks truth amid lies and deception.

THE SPIRIT OF TRUTH:

25 I have told you all these things while I am with you. 26 But the Helper will teach you everything and will cause you to remember all that I told you. This Helper is the Holy Spirit, whom the Father will send in my name. **John 14:25-26 (NCV)**

As human beings we are subject to a lot of falsehood and deception because of three fundamental weaknesses in human character:

1. We want to believe what we think is best for us.
2. We are easily persuaded to a flawed point of view.
3. We are driven by such social needs as acceptability and the need to belong.

The Holy Spirit teaches us from the point of view of Christ. The Word and our contact and experience with Christ contain his teachings. The Holy Spirit's instructions are both personal and practical.

CONCLUSION:

An old hymn tells us that we have a friend in Jesus. When we look at the personal role of the Holy Spirit, we quickly conclude that he is also our friend. It is up to us to get to know him better as he ministers to us. I think we can all look forward to experiencing what the Holy Spirit has for us.

NOTES:

28

THE HOLY SPIRIT AS GOD'S OIL

INTRODUCTION

Today we will examine the symbol of oil to see what it can tell us about the Holy Spirit. Of all the generations of believers that have passed, ours has a unique understanding of the importance of oil. If all the oil fields were to dry up suddenly, our global technical civilization would come to a grinding halt. Oil today is justly known as "black gold" and as a fossil fuel is of higher value than gold.

The fact that natural oil is of high value, tells us something about the oil of the Holy Spirit. Without that precious oil of the Spirit, our personal and corporate spiritual lives will also come to a screeching stop.

Without the oil of the Holy Spirit, the world, the flesh, and the Devil would dry us out and burn us up. So, we need to understand some of the fundamental ways that we need the oil of the Spirit in our lives.

THE OIL THAT BEAUTIFIES AND HEALS:

The oil of the Bible is not our familiar fossil fuel but came from living plants, primarily crushed olives.

There are 12 types of oils mentioned in the Bible. The oils are of two kinds. Oils which contained fats, and fat-free oils. The fat-free oils were used to beautify and heal the people - they were fragrant and costly.

1. Aloes/Sandalwood.
2. Cassia.
3. Cedarwood.
4. Cypress.
5. Frankincense.
6. Galbanum.
7. Hyssop.
8. Myrrh.
9. Myrtle.
10. Onycha. (Exodus 30:34)
11. Rose of Sharon/Cistus.
12. Spikenard.

THE OIL THAT BEAUTIFIES:

³and provide for those who grieve in Zion— to bestow on them a crown of beauty instead of ashes, the oil of gladness instead of mourning, and a garment of praise instead of a spirit of despair. **Isaiah 61: 3 (NIV)**

The Holy Spirit is beautiful.
- The Holy Spirit who lives in you makes you beautiful in your spirit. He gives you the oil of joy.
- If you look at each other with spiritual eyes, you will see the inner beauty that Christians share.
- To see this beauty in each other is to glorify the source - Jesus Christ.
- To see this beauty in yourself is to positively and permanently change your self-image.
- To know that you are beautiful in Christ is to show the world his beauty from your ashes.

THE OIL THAT HEALS:

¹⁴Anyone who is sick should call the church's elders. They should pray for and pour oil on the person£ in the name of the Lord. ¹⁵And the prayer that is said with faith will make the sick person well; the Lord will heal that person. And if the person has sinned, the sins will be forgiven. **James 5:14-15 (NCV)**

Each of the 12 oils I mentioned, including olive oil, was used as a medicine for healing. These oils share real healing properties. For example, the Good Samaritan poured oil on the wounds of the man he found beaten on the road to Jericho. (Luke 10:34).

- The Holy Spirit is our healer and the source of the gift of healing mentioned in I Corinthians 12.
- The healing oil of the Spirit symbolizes the power of the Holy Spirit.

So, in chapter 5 of the Book of James, pouring oil on the person represents pouring the power of the Holy Spirit upon the person, and it is that power that heals the person.

THE OIL THAT PROVIDES LIGHT:

[20]*"Command the people of Israel to bring you pure olive oil, made from pressed olives, to keep the lamps on the lamp stand burning. [21]Aaron and his sons must keep the lamps burning before the LORD from evening till morning. This will be in the Meeting Tent, outside the curtain which is in front of the Ark. The Israelites and their descendants must obey this rule from now on.* **Exodus 27:20-21 (NCV)**

Most of the time when the Bible mentions oil, it is referring to olive oil.

- The Old Testament commanded that only olive oil is used to burn in lamps. (Exodus 25:6).
- The tent of God, the tabernacle of David, and the Temple were enclosed and dark. Certainly, the temple had no windows in the sanctuary and the Holy of Holies, so the only light came from the lamp described in Zechariah 4:2.
- We are the temple of God. We are the sanctuary of God, and the Holy Spirit is the source of light for our inner spiritual man.
- That light keeps us from the darkness and reassures us that God is present within us and that he shall never leave us or abandon us.
- It is the oil of the Holy Spirit that enables us to be the "light of the world." (Matthew 5:14)
- The lamp before the altar was intended to have a flame which never went out, the Holy Spirit burns brightly within us for eternity and eternally present with us.

Even so, we can neglect the flame burning within us by ignoring the Holy Spirit and the gifts he gives us. Jesus was very clear about this in his story of ten bridesmaids.

[1]" At that time the kingdom of heaven will be like ten bridesmaids who took their lamps and went to wait for the bridegroom. [2]Five of them were foolish and five were wise. [3]The five foolish bridesmaids took their lamps, but they did not take more oil for the lamps to burn. [4]The wise bridesmaids took their lamps and more oil in jars. [5]Because the bridegroom was late, they became sleepy and went to sleep. [6]" At midnight someone cried out, 'The bridegroom is coming! Come and meet him!' [7]Then all the bridesmaids woke up and got their lamps ready. [8]But the foolish ones said to the wise, 'Give us some of your oil, because our lamps are going out. [9]The wise bridesmaids answered, 'No, the oil we have might not be enough for all of us. Go to the people who sell oil and buy some for yourselves.' [10]"So while the five foolish bridesmaids went to buy oil, the bridegroom came. The bridesmaids who were ready went in with the bridegroom to the wedding feast. Then the door was closed and locked. [11]"Later the others came back and said, 'Sir, sir, open the door to let us in. [12]But the bridegroom answered, 'I tell you the truth, I don't want to know you.' [13]"So always be ready, because you don't know the day or the hour the Son of Man will come. **Matthew 25:1-13 (NCV)**

- I pray that you will never shout out "my lamp is going out."
- You need to be prepared by being continually filled with the oil of the Holy Spirit.
- You need to be constantly aware that your lamp will burn brightly for eternity if you draw from the Holy Spirit.

THE OIL THAT ANOINTS FOR SERVICE TO JESUS CHRIST:
The Bible speaks of anointing over 150 times.
- It tells us that there were anointed priests, kings, and prophets.
- To Christians, the anointing of the Holy Spirit is both confirmation of a call and enablement to serve in that call.
- The anointing oil is like God's declaration that the person is ready to represent him to the world. It is like God's signature and a seal on our service to him.
- In fact, the Holy Spirit is called God's seal on our lives, and so each of us has an anointing. *[1]Now it is God who makes both us and you stand firm in Christ. He anointed us, [22]set his seal of*

ownership on us, and put his Spirit in our hearts as a deposit, guaranteeing what is to come **2 Corinthians 1:21-22(NIV)**

- We must not minister outside of our anointing, and so we must be careful to wait for clear guidance from the Holy Spirit.
- It is a severe mistake to leap ahead or lag behind the anointing of the Holy Spirit. Both suggest a lack of readiness to serve him.

CONCLUSION

Let us always remember that the oil of anointing is for us. Let us always seek the anointing of the Holy Spirit to proclaim the mighty acts of God through the oil of the Holy Spirit. Let us be both obedient and faithful to his call to serve with authentic passion and devotion. The world needs healing both physically and spiritually. Let us remain close to the healer. It is only the Holy Spirit who can help us.

NOTES:

THE FIRE OF PENTECOST

²⁹

Text: ¹*When the day of Pentecost came, they were all together in one place. ²Suddenly a noise like a strong, blowing wind came from heaven and filled the whole house where they were sitting. ³They saw something like flames of fire that were separated and stood over each person there. ⁴They were all filled with the Holy Spirit, and they began to speak different languages by the power the Holy Spirit was giving them.* **Acts 2:1-4 (NCV)**

INTRODUCTION:

God never does anything without purpose or meaning. In the Spirit-filled church of today we see some of the manifestations that happened at Pentecost, but not all of them. One not replicated to date is that of fire, or rather the Holy Spirit power that is like fire. Perhaps if we understand how God uses this power, we can understand more about its purpose.

FIRE IN THE OLD TESTAMENT:

While the fire of Pentecost was a new thing that God did for the believers in Christ, we can see foreshadows of it in the Old Testament. For example, the fire seen by Moses:

¹*One day Moses was taking care of Jethro's flock. (Jethro was the priest of Midian and also Moses' father-in-law.) When Moses led the flock to the west side of the desert, he came to Sinai, the mountain of God. ²There the angel of the LORD appeared to him in flames of fire coming out of a bush. Moses saw that the bush was on fire, but it was not burning up. ³So he said, "I will go closer to this strange thing. How can a bush continue burning without burning up?"* **Exodus 3:1-3 (NCV)**

God had something to say and used the appearance of fire to attract attention to what was happening.

- In both cases, the flame only appeared to be fire. It was likely some form of energy which did not consume the bush and which seemed to be "something like flames of fire" at Pentecost.
- In both cases, there was an impartation of power. For Moses to lead Israel out of captivity, and for the disciples to preach the Gospel to the whole world by establishing the church.
- It provided guidance and direction. Like the cloud of fire in Exodus:
  [38]So the cloud of the LORD was over the Holy Tent during the day, and there was a fire in the cloud at night. So all the Israelites could see the cloud while they travel. **Exodus 40:38 (NCV)**
- Fire in the cloud illuminated the darkness and gave direction. The fire of the Baptism of the Holy Spirit equipped the apostles to penetrate the darkness in the world.
- The fire upon the apostles became the fire in the apostles and the world was changed because it had a new direction of travel - the "way" of Christ.

The fire of Pentecost was also symbolic of God acting. Mindful of the several cases of "fire out of heaven." Two types of circumstances brought fire out of heaven. The first was God's judgment meant to punish and destroy while the second was to accept an offering and bless (2 Chronicles 7:1 Solomon).

- The fire out of heaven during Pentecost was acceptance of the disciples because of Jesus.
- The fire out of heaven during Pentecost was a blessing - a direct empowering of the disciples. It is no coincidence that they experienced tongues of fire followed by tongues of praise.

CONCLUSION:

Today when we get the Baptism of the Holy Spirit, we do not see tongues of fire. We do get fired up though by the enabling power of the Holy Spirit. We still hear the tongues of praise and get fired up in our spirits. Perhaps we do not see the fire out of heaven, but it is still there whenever anyone gets baptized in the Holy Spirit.

NOTES:

30

THE BARNABAS
MINISTRY

Text: *³⁶Joseph, a Levite from Cyprus, whom the apostles called
Barnabas (which means Son of Encouragement)* **Acts 4:36 (NIV)**

INTRODUCTION:
In this sermon, I would like to discuss the Barnabas ministry, a
ministry which is vital for the church. As indicated by our Scripture
for today, Joseph was a Levite who regularly attended the church in
Jerusalem. Joseph seemed to have the ability to console, comfort,
and encourage the people of the church. This ability was a ministry
of Joseph's; acknowledged by the apostles, and as a result, they gave
him the title of "Barnabas" which spoke to Joseph's character and
gifts through the Holy Spirit.

A ministry of encouragement is as vital to the church today as it has
been in the past. I also believe that there are people among us who
have a Barnabas ministry that is yet to be developed and applied in
the church, and I hope that this sermon will encourage them to begin
to implement their ministry for the benefit of the church. So, we must
discuss what type of ministry activities that Barnabas showed to us,
particularly in the Book of Acts.

TO HELP PEOPLE INTEGRATE INTO THE CHURCH:
Whenever visitors come to a church, they must overcome obstacles
and barriers that might prevent them from either returning to church
or joining it. The Devil delights in causing visitors to feel rejected

or offended when they visit a new church. Resolving offense is a primary area for someone with a Barnabas ministry. In fact, we see this ministry of Barnabas taking place with Saul, who was to become Paul.

For example [26] *When he came to Jerusalem, he tried to join the disciples, but they were all afraid of him, not believing that he really was a disciple.* [27]*But Barnabas took him and brought him to the apostles. He told them how Saul on his journey had seen the Lord and that the Lord had spoken to him, and how in Damascus he had preached fearlessly in the name of Jesus.* [28]*So Saul stayed with them and moved about freely in Jerusalem, speaking boldly in the name of the Lord.* **Acts 9:26 – 28 (NIV)**

- Paul had persecuted the church, and there was absolutely no reason to believe that he converted to Christianity.
- It could be that his alleged conversion was a deception so that he could get more information about Christians to persecute them.
- Barnabas believed Paul and gave testimony about his conversion. He recommended that the apostles accept Paul as part of the church.
- In the same way, the Barnabas ministry in the church urges people to become members or to faithfully attend services because the church needs them and they need the church.
- The Barnabas minister will also offer consolation and comfort and will reach out to establish relationships with visitors to the church.
- The Barnabas minister will attempt to resolve conflicts within the church to help people stay in the church.
- The Barnabas minister will also reassure all who visit that they are welcome and not judged in any manner

THE SPIRITUAL GIFTS INVOLVED WITH THE BARNABAS MINISTRY:

The Barnabas ministry is not just a social ministry. It also uses several of the spiritual gifts. For example:

- The gift of discernment: This gift may lead the Barnabas minister to visitors that are having difficulty with the church service or who may have been offended. Through this gift, the Barnabas minister will discern who needs his ministry after the service ends. Of course, for this gift to be useful, the Barnabas minister must be alert to visitors and the voice of the Holy Spirit.

- The gift of knowledge: If a visitor or church member is upset, the Barnabas minister must have some idea as to what happened or at the very least why the person is angry. The Holy Spirit will provide the necessary information for the Barnabas minister to understand the issues involved. In other words, the gift of knowledge will provide information needed for ministry to those who are feeling offended, rejected, fearful, or confused.

- The gift of wisdom: The gift of wisdom will tell the Barnabas minister exactly how to minister to the people that he knows need ministry, and according to the information he has about what is required during ministry. In other words, the Holy Spirit will give the person supernatural wisdom to deal with the issues.

What the Barnabas minister says, how he brings comfort, the degree to which he understands the issue, and how he establishes a relationship with others is all naturally and easily guided by the Holy Spirit. The comfort offered along with compassion and empathy flow as a natural part of this ministry without stress or strain. In fact, the minister may be surprised at how quickly and how well his ministry progresses as he reaches out to the people at church.

THE BARNABAS MINISTER AS A COUNSELOR:

A word of encouragement can have a profound positive effect on the life of a struggling Christian. Barnabas demonstrated this ministry with Mark. In the Book of Acts 15:37 – 41 we see the struggle of Mark as he failed Paul during the first missionary journey. Paul is not willing to give Mark another chance to redeem himself, but Barnabas believed in Mark in the same way that he believed in Paul. Barnabas stood by Mark even if it meant separating himself from Paul. Barnabas took Mark along with him on his missionary trip to help Mark mature and be encouraged in the service of the Lord.

- The Barnabas minister will console and encourage those who are having difficulty in ministry. This encouragement can take the form of simple counseling involving appreciation, compassion, and understanding of the problems the troubled minister is facing.

- The Barnabas ministry is filled with mercy and forgiveness so that those who have fallen can find strength and determination to go on in their ministry field.
- The Barnabas minister will go out of his way to keep the sheep in the shepherd's pasture rather than letting them wander away and become victims to the wolves of life.

CONCLUSION:

Is there a Barnabas hiding in you? The church needs people like Barnabas who care and are willing to minister to visitors and other church members with comfort, consolation, and sympathy. If you feel that you could participate as a Barnabas minister, then look around for those who need your ministry.

NOTES:

31

HEAVEN

Text: *¹Jesus said, "Don't let your hearts be troubled. Trust in God, and trust in me. ²There are many rooms in my Father's house; I would not tell you this if it were not true. I am going there to prepare a place for you. ³After I go and prepare a place for you; I will come back and take you to be with me so that you may be where I am.* **John 14:1-3 (NCV)**

INTRODUCTION:

Jesus promised us that he would come back for us and take us to a place called heaven. In both the Greek and Hebrew languages, heaven means "sky." The natural sky consists of the atmosphere and outer space, but the Biblical reference to sky denotes the place where God lives and where he has his throne (Psalms 2:4). It is a place that Jesus returned to after his resurrection (Acts 1:11); where the church triumphant unites for worship (Hebrews 12:22 – 25) and where one day we will be with Jesus forever. In this sermon, I'd like to discuss some of the characteristics of heaven.

CHARACTERISTICS OF HEAVEN:

Scripture tends to define heaven by the effects and benefits that it has on those who go there. We know that it is the place where we experience the unreserved presence of God, and we will see the glorified Christ. We also know that it is the place that the church worships Christ and our final destination, the place of light and closeness to God. Scripture tells us about some of the other characteristics of heaven such as:

- Heaven is a place for us to go. (John 14:2)
- Heaven is a city. (Hebrews 11:10)
- Heaven is a country. (Hebrews 11: 16)

- Heaven is a new cosmos. (Revelations 21:1).
- Heaven is a holy place, and all those in it are holy.

DISTINCTIONS:
Scripture draws distinctions that we must keep in mind if we are going to try to understand heaven. These distinctions are:
- The heavenly world mentioned in Ephesians 6, is different than heaven. Hostile spiritual powers, demons, and lost souls occupy the heavenly realms.
- While we are in our physical bodies, we do not easily experience heaven because it is invisible and we can know about it only by faith.
- Heaven is nevertheless a reality. It is the place where the Father, Son, and Holy Spirit along with the angels abide even today, even now, and is very close to us – just a breath away.

BENEFITS OF HEAVEN:
On lives in heaven will be substantially different than our lives in this world.
- An essential idea concerning heaven is that we will not be limited by the imperfections of our present relationship with God and with the cosmos. We will be able to deal with the cosmos and the physical universe in substantially different ways.
- In heaven, we will be in touching distance from God! We will freely serve him, and we will be in command of the cosmos in the process of serving him.
- The feelings and problems which presently produce both physical and emotional limitations, such as pain, conflicts, and suffering, will not exist in heaven.
- Scripture seems to indicate that we will be in constant joy when we are in heaven.

OUR JOY IN HEAVEN:
The joy that we will experience in heaven stems from some specific conditions and blessings that we will have when we are with Christ.
- Our understanding and experience of Christ will be exponentially expanded, and that will bring us great joy.

- In heaven, we will have a direct and continuous experience of Christ's love for us as he ministers to us in a way we have never experienced before.
- We will be in contact with our loved ones and have fellowship with the whole body of Christ.
- While in heaven we will continue to grow, mature, learn and develop new abilities as we serve him with extended spiritual gifts that God has for us.

CONCLUSION:

The heavenly glory that we will experience is a result of seeing God in and through Christ. We will also be loved by the Father, the Son, and the Holy Spirit without the uncertainty and doubt that may torment us now. We will have work to do for our Lord and Savior and will praise and worship him continually. We will also rejoice in the fellowship that we have with the redeemed. Heaven then is a place that we can look forward to entering after we finish this life. It is a place that we will be rewarded for our good works, although perhaps the most magnificent reward will be the pure passion and intensity of our love for God and his love for us.

NOTES:

32

THE LIVING CHURCH

Text: *²⁷Together you are the body of Christ, and each one of you is a part of that body.* **1 Corinthians 12:27 (NCV)**

INTRODUCTION

What is the church? Why is it so important to Christ that he died for it, and declared that the power of hell would not overcome it? Throughout the ages, the concept of the church has changed as society changes. There are a few principles that have not changed, and those basic ideas about the church must be protected and remain current, age through age.

WHAT THE CHURCH IS NOT:

The church is not an organization. While the church is organized, its nature is far beyond simple social structure.

- The church is not like a business, a social club, or our government. Ironically, it has characteristics of each of these, but its primary purpose is different from these.
- The church has been called an army, a kingdom, a place of worship, a holy place, and a congregation of believers. But these descriptions only take into consideration a part of the whole nature of the church.

WHAT IS THE CHURCH?

Scientists have begun to redefine what it means to be a living entity. For example, some scientists have started to think that cities are living entities. They have the equivalent of blood vessels in their highways, a nervous system in their electrical wiring, a central coordinating area equivalent to a brain in their governmental structure.

- A long time before anyone postulated these radical scientific ideas, Paul describes the church as the living body of Christ. He said that the church is a living being.
- If we comprehend the nature of the church as a living being, we come to a new understanding of its purpose and destiny.

THE NATURE OF THIS LIVING CHURCH:

⁴Each one of us has a body with many parts, and these parts all have different uses. ⁵In the same way, we are many, but in Christ we are all one body. Each one is a part of that body, and each part belongs to all the other parts. **Romans 12:4-5 (NCV)**

- The church consists of saved individuals united together in love for a specific purpose.
- Love is the glue that holds the church together. If you do not have love in the church, you do not have the church even though you might have a vast organization.
- That is why Scripture says that you shall know them by their love. By their agape love.
- This love means that we belong to Christ and that we belong to each other. We become a family.
- If we belong to each other, then we should take care of each other. This means we should nurture each other, help provide for each other, protect each other, support each other, accept each other, and work together.

¹⁶The whole body depends on Christ, and all the parts of the body are joined and held together. Each part does its own work to make the whole body grow and be strong with love. **Ephesians 4:16 (NCV)**

- The head of the church is Christ. The great danger occurs when men try to be the head of the church instead of Christ. Unless Christ is the head, you have no church.
- Each of us depends on Christ, and we all together must also rely on him because it is through the Holy Spirit that we join together.
- Each person in the church has a job. That job is to increase the love that we have for Christ and each other. A church

which is divided is a church in which the people are not doing their job.

^{14}More and more men and women believed in the Lord and were added to the group of believers. **Acts 5:14 (NCV)**

The church should not grow by division, but the church should increase by addition.
- Addition takes place when profound personal changes take place in individuals as they meet Christ through the witness of the body.
- It is important to realize that Jesus did not change society by changing its organizations, its religions, or the government. He changed the entire world, one person at a time.

^{1}Jesus was going through the city of Jericho ^{2}A man was there named Zacchaeus, who was a very important tax collector, and he was wealthy. ^{3}He wanted to see who Jesus was, but he was not able because he was too short to see above the crowd. ^{4}He ran ahead to a place where Jesus would come, and he climbed a sycamore tree so he could see him. ^{5}When Jesus came to that place, he looked up and said to him, "Zacchaeus, hurry and come down! I must stay at your house today." ^{6}Zacchaeus came down quickly and welcomed him gladly. ^{7}All the people saw this and began to complain, "Jesus is staying with a sinner!" ^{8}But Zacchaeus stood and said to the Lord, "I will give half of my possessions to the poor. And if I have cheated anyone, I will pay back four times more." ^{9}Jesus said to him, "Salvation has come to this house today because this man also belongs to the family of Abraham. ^{10}The Son of Man came to find lost people and save them." **Luke 19:1-10 (NCV)**
- Zacharias was despised because he was a tax collector.
- People thought less of Jesus because Jesus sought out someone who was a despicable person according to popular opinion.
- He did not judge Zacchaeus but accepted him for who he was. Zacchaeus already knew about his sins, so Jesus did not have to point them out or even remind him of his sins.

- Jesus did not try to change the tax collection system; he did change the tax collector.
- Jesus said that he came to search for and save such as these and that is the mission of the church and the mission of all of us collectively together.

TO CONTINUE TO LIVE THE CHURCH NEEDS UNITY:

[10]I beg you, brothers and sisters, by the name of our Lord Jesus Christ that all of you agree with each other and not be split into groups. I beg that you be completely joined together by having the same kind of thinking and the same purpose. **1 Corinthians 1:10 (NCV)**

- Division and discord are two weapons the Devil uses to paralyze the church and weaken it.
- Almost all division and dissension come from offense, and the offense is rooted in pride.
- Pride separates individuals from each other based on the source of pride. The source can be social status, money, or favoritism.
- Agreeing about what we think does not mean we all hold the same opinion. It means that we have a consensus which is in line with the mission of Christ.
- Having the same purpose does not mean we have the same methodology, for example, contemporary versus traditional worship.
- There's nothing wrong with small groups who have unity with the whole church, but beware of a divisive group.

SUPPORT:

[24]Let us think about each other and help each other to show love and do good deeds. [25]You should not stay away from the church meetings, as some are doing, but you should meet together and encourage each other. Do this even more as you see the day coming. **Hebrews 10:24-25 (NCV)**

- Support means that you recognize your importance to other people.
- When you attend church, you are not only worshiping God, but you're supporting your brothers and sisters who need you.

- The Devil hates it when you support your church! You should realize that he will do anything within his power to keep you from attending church.
- Your presence is an encouragement to church members and pastors.
- As we experience more oppression and discrimination as Christians, we should pull tightly together in the harmony of one spirit, one body, and one Savior.

FAITHFULNESS:

[13] *"You are the salt of the earth. But if the salt loses its salty taste, it cannot be made salty again. It is good for nothing, except to be thrown out and walked on.* **Matthew 5:13 (NCV)**

- Faithfulness means that we remain true to who we are, or rather who Christ wants us to be.
- Faithfulness means that we do not compromise biblical standards under societal pressure.
- Faithfulness means that we bring all the promises of Christ into the world, but do not become like the world.
- Faithfulness means that we stay true to the ministry of Christ and the mission of Christ.
- Faithfulness means that we stay connected and obedient to the head of the church and to what he determines he wants to be done by his body.

CONCLUSION:

If someone tells you that they are Christian, but do not believe in the church, then you are most likely looking at an ineffective Christian that lacks love. Be sure to tell him that Christ not only died for him but also for the church. After all, the church is people who believe in Christ, and they all are brothers and sisters in the Lord.

NOTES:

33

UNDERSTANDING THE UNCHURCHED

Text: *²⁵You should not stay away from the church meetings, as some are doing, but you should meet together and encourage each other. Do this even more as you see the day coming.* **Hebrews 10:25 (NCV)**

THE FORCE OF CULTURE:

In the last 100 years, there has emerged three philosophies, which have become incorporated into our culture and which have diminished the need to be part of the church.

1. Secularism, which attempts to eliminate religion from public life. (Church is not wanted.)
2. Individualism, which reinforces the idea that religion is a private matter differing for everyone according to that person's opinion. (Church is not needed.)
3. Religious Freedom, which has come to mean freedom from worship rather than freedom to worship. (Church is not necessary.)

These forces have produced profound cultural changes over the years.

- Sunday was once considered a holy day instead of a holiday. Now we have many competitive activities to steal our loyalty to the church.
- Sunday was once considered a day of rest and worship, not a work day. Now many companies require their employees to work on Sunday. They are expected to work regardless of the

adverse spiritual effects occurred by not worshiping God and being a church member.
- The church was once considered a place of help and support instead of an entertainment center.

WHY SHOULD THEY COME?

What value does the church have for our visitors? Why should they come back? Why should someone who would rather be playing golf, attend church instead?
- People are helped to deal with life because they learned something about their faith from the sermon. The sermon feeds the spirits of the people! Some do not absorb the sermon because they have an eating disorder such as unforgiving hearts, anger, bitterness, or egotism.
- Visitors need to feel loved, welcomed, and needed by the body of Christ. They need to be told that they are welcome.
- Do visitors feel forgiveness and new life from the church as a whole? They need to be accepted!
- Do they know the church needs them? They need to be put into service!

NOT RESPONSIBLE:

The church is not responsible for people who leave because they:
- Object to the fact that the church is open to all races and all people from all walks of life, including those with shady backgrounds and questionable pasts.
- Object to the move of the Holy Spirit and his manifestations among his people such as speaking in tongues or the other gifts.
- They cannot stand a strong and correcting word from the pastor or preacher.
- The presence and power of the Holy Spirit are so strong that it makes them want to run away from him.

REASONS:

Some reasons that people give for not attending or leaving a church are:

- They felt rejected. This rejection may be an imaginary offense based on a false assumption. When you visit a church that you have never been to before, you are nervous and tense because you do not know what to expect. In such situations, it is easy to be offended, perhaps because no one made you feel at home and wanted in the church. To overcome this problem, visitors must know that we care about them. Simple friendliness is a start.
- They felt neglected. People must know that we will try to meet their needs as best we can.
- They were in disunity. We must tell people that we are loyal to them, and we expect them to be faithful to us. (Especially leadership)
- They were used and abused. Love not condemnation or judgment must rule our hearts. *24Let us think about each other and help each other to show love and do good deeds.* **Hebrews 10:24 (NCV)**

CONCLUSION:

Why do people desperately need the church?
- In a world full of entertainment through radio, movies, television, and the internet, only in the church can they find true community worship.
- In a world driven by diverse philosophies and religions, only in the church will they learn the truth, the way, and the life.
- In a world filled with distracting activities only through the church will they find service blessed by the Lord.
- Only through the church will they find preparation for their final place in the glory of God's kingdom.

NOTES:

34

BASIC DISCIPLESHIP

Text: *[15]Jesus said to his followers, "Go everywhere in the world, and tell the Good News to everyone.* **Mark 16:15 (NCV)**

INTRODUCTION:

The plan of salvation is not complicated. God kept it simple because he wanted it to be inclusive. People can understand what it takes to be saved just by hearing or reading the Word of God. If a church is living, then people are being saved through its ministries. Once people make that all-important commitment to Jesus, they need to not only understand what has happened to them, but they also need to know what steps they must take to grow and mature as Christians. In this sermon, I will outline some of the understandings that a new convert needs to have and the steps he needs to take to make progress as a Christian.

EFFECTS OF SALVATION:

Your new convert has committed to Jesus. You have told him that he needs Christ if his sins are to be forgiven and if he wants to go to heaven. Whether he "feels" different or not, there are three things he needs to know about the impact of salvation on his life;

- New Life: Every person has a soul consisting of a body, mind, and spirit. So, every human being has a spirit. Before salvation that spirit is separated from spiritual life in God and so is functionally dead. That dead spirit still exists but has no connection with God because of original sin. After salvation occurs, that spirit is connected to the God of life and begins to function. In truth, the spirit has been "born again" as Jesus said: *⁷Don't be surprised when I tell you, 'You must all be born again.'* **John 3:7 (NCV)** The human spirit begins to change the mind and influence the body of the saved person. The saved person has moved from spiritual death to eternal life in Christ.

- New Creation: The born-again Christian is referred to as a new creation since all aspects of his life have changed by the re-birth of his spirit. The new creation means that salvation makes us new people no longer in bondage to our past lifestyle of sin. Once saved, human nature changes. The Christian life is an adventure of exploring and growing in our new life, and the Bible is our tour guide. The new person has a sincere desire to read and live by the Bible to please God.

- New Hope*: In God's great mercy he has caused us to be born again into a living hope, because Jesus Christ rose from the dead. ⁴Now we hope for the blessings God has for his children.* **1Peter 1:3-4 (NCV)** The new convert now understands that he has been given new life, that he is a new person, and now he has new hope for his life. This hope includes not only his eventual resurrection but also his daily life in Christ. He will begin to understand the Bible, learn how to pray, be of service to others, and witness to the lost about Christ. All this will result in treasures stored in heaven that he can look forward to as he comes to the end of his life.

WATER BAPTISM:

While salvation comes from making a faith commitment to Jesus, water baptism is an essential step he needs to take as part of the salvation experience. Jesus commanded every believer to be water baptized when he said: *¹⁶Anyone who believes and is baptized will be saved, but anyone who does not believe will be punished.* **Mark 16:16 (NCV).** (Please note that in this verse, salvation results from belief, not water.) The new convert may not know why water baptism is so essential and so you need to give him the following information:

- Water baptism is a public commitment to follow Christ. It is an action taken to state that he is saved through Jesus, but also that Jesus is his Lord. Since Jesus is his Lord, the convert will do as Jesus commands, go where Jesus tells him to go, and serve as Jesus gives him a ministry.

- Water baptism is also a recognition that the convert's sinful lifestyle is "washed away" and that he is now a new person with a new life ahead of him.
- Water baptism is symbolic of the death and resurrection of Christ. Water baptism is a step which declares the resurrection of all believers after death. It is a statement that while our lives end in death, we will continue to live with Christ, and will experience resurrection.

BAPTISM OF THE HOLY SPIRIT:

Before the Lord went to heaven, he promised us that believers would be empowered by the Holy Spirit when he said: *⁸But when the Holy Spirit comes to you, you will receive power.* **Acts 1:8 (NCV).** While many Christian denominations ignore this promise, or reject it because they believe that it does not apply to modern believers, the new convert needs to know the following about the Baptism of the Holy Spirit:

- Every believer receives the Holy Spirit when conversion takes place. (John 20:22) but the Baptism in the Holy Spirit means that the believer is empowered by the Holy Spirit to work in the spiritual gifts mentioned in 1 Corinthians 12.
- The Baptism of the Holy Spirit is an experience that allows better evangelism by demonstrating the gifts of the Spirit to non-believers.
- The Baptism of the Holy Spirit empowers better service because the gifts function for the common good of church members. (1 Corinthians 12:7)
- The Baptism of the Holy Spirit elevates daily disciplines of the Christian. For example, instead of praying from his mind, the Christian baptized with the Spirit can pray with his spirit to the Spirit of God. Also, counseling is made more potent through the gifts of wisdom, and knowledge. The Word of God has a more significant impact because the Holy Spirit can bring new and exciting meanings to the scriptures.

FELLOWSHIP:

The new convert should be encouraged to attend and then join a church. He needs to belong where Jesus sends him for the following reasons:

- We are commanded to meet together so that we can encourage each other. (Hebrews 10:25)
- The church can become a support group helping the new convert change.
- The church is a place to grow and mature as the convert learns how to forgive and love.
- The church is a place to serve the Lord and earn the rewards of service.
- The church is a safe place where the convert can trust church leaders and learn to please God.

DAILY DISCIPLINES:

Daily disciplines are those steps and actions that the new convert needs to incorporate in his spiritual life. Examples of three of these daily disciplines include:

1. Integrating the Word: The Bible is God's book of guidelines to living a happy and productive Christian life. While reading the Bible is good, just reading or even memorizing it is not enough. The convert must start believing and living according to what he reads in the Bible if it is to have a good effect.
2. Prayer: Once the convert has a relationship with Jesus, he needs to start talking (praying) to Jesus every day by spending some time praising and worshipping Jesus, discussing issues with Jesus, and giving thanks to Jesus. Time must be set aside for prayer, and the habit of prayer established.
3. Witnessing: Whether a Christian is a new believer or an old timer, the need to witness about salvation by example and evangelism should be a constant practice.

CONCLUSION:

When a person is saved, there is a need to understand what happened at their conversion. They need to grasp the spiritual power and wonder of what occurred when they believed in Christ. They need to know the steps they must take to grow and mature. They need to be loved by the church and learn to love others in the church. To merely pray the sinner's prayer and then abandon them is irresponsible and detrimental to their welfare.

NOTES:

35

THREE ASPECTS
OF EVANGELISM

Text: *³⁷Jesus said to his followers, "There are many people to harvest but only a few workers to help harvest them. ³⁸Pray to the Lord, who owns the harvest, that he will send more workers to gather his harvest*
Matthew 9:37-38 (NCV)

INTRODUCTION
As we look at the world today, we see Christian morals, values, and influence vastly diminishing. We are losing more and more people to false religions and to atheism than ever before. If Christians diminish in numbers in our country, then they are also diminishing in political influence. Indeed, religious hatred and discrimination are not new to Christianity, but they are new to Christians in this country. Many say that we are a post-Christian nation. That means that the prevalence and popularity of the Christian faith are no longer vital or essential to our country. The question is, how should we react to this sad state of affairs?

REACTIONS TO AVOID:
We could react with defeat and give up the fight. Believing that our situation is hopeless and that we are helpless, we could withdraw into ourselves and refuse to witness to anyone because we think that it is useless to do so. Other options are possible for us:
- We could hide in our righteousness while condemning the world to hell.
- We could become militant about our faith and attempt to force people to become Christians.

- We could blame God for everything and by doing so avoid any responsibility that we might have for the salvation of others.
- We could come to believe that the Devil has got the victory and is more predominant and accepted today than in previous times

None of these reactions are useful or helpful because they don't deal with the problem. They don't explain why we are falling behind in the conversion of people to Christ.

THE SOLUTION:

We may have forgotten that Matthew expresses the essential nature of the great commission:

[18]Then Jesus came to them and said, "All power in heaven and on earth is given to me. [19]So go and make followers of all people in the world. Baptize them in the name of the Father and the Son and the Holy Spirit. [20]Teach them to obey everything that I have taught you, and I will be with you always, even until the end of this age." **Matthew 28:18-20 (NCV)**

- The last thing that Christ said to his followers is to make disciples of all nations. For him and us today that must be the top priority of our work and purpose.
- As soon as we substitute church programs, entertainment, fellowship, or even worship for the great commission we are walking in disobedience.
- As soon as we minimize the role of the Holy Spirit, who is the great evangelist, in the church and our lives, we walk in a lack of submission to the purposes of God to save the world.
- Finally, when we miss the heart of Christ in evangelism, we become ineffective and inefficient.

THE HEART OF CHRIST:

When we look at the heart of Christ, we see several significant characteristics that we also must have to win the world. These characteristics are compassion, communication, and service.

COMPASSION:

[36]When he saw the crowds, he had compassion for them, because they were harassed and helpless, **Matthew 9:36 (NIV)**

It's remarkable how little human nature has changed in 2000 years. We look at nation after nation and see that the people of those countries are just as harassed and as helpless as they were during the time of Christ.

- When people were hurting and in pain from sicknesses, Christ was moved by compassion to heal them. (Matthew 14:14).
- When people were in the grasp of demons, Christ was moved by compassion to deliver them. (Mark 9:22).
- When people experienced human sorrow and grief, Christ was moved by compassion to comfort them even to the point of raising the dead. (Luke 7:11 -- 15).
- Jesus was moved with compassion because people suffered from hunger. (Matthew 15:32).
- Jesus was moved with compassion for people that were suffering from loneliness and isolation. (Mark 1:41)
- Finally, Jesus was moved with compassion for people who were lost and condemned to spend eternity in separation from God and all that is good.

You can't efficiently witness with a hardened heart full of judgment. Your heart must flow with understanding, empathy, and love for those who are suffering, helpless, and lost. To witness without compassion, just for the sake of witnessing is useless and will win no one to the heart of Christ. Compassion must take hold of us so that we see beyond the external into the depths of the souls of the lost. Compassion is as important as obedience and surrender.

COMMUNICATION:

Who owns the harvest? (Vs. 38)

- In my opinion, the Holy Spirit owns the harvest.
- The Holy Spirit empowers us to evangelize. Without the active role played by the Holy Spirit, salvation is not possible.
- This places emphasis on the Baptism of the Holy Spirit by which Christians are empowered to be witnesses and to model for the world to live the walk of Christ.
- The fewer Christians that have the Baptism of the Holy Spirit, the weaker Christianity becomes. We are losing the world because we are not connected to and communicating with the Spirit of God.

- We are to "ask" the Lord, and that implies two-way communication. Asking means receiving so not only do we need to ask the Holy Spirit who, how, and when to evangelize, but we need to listen to his answers as well. Conversely, the more Christians baptized in the Holy Spirit, the stronger Christianity becomes.

SERVICE:

...he will send more workers to gather his harvest (Vs. 38)

In the Greek, the word "send" has a stronger meaning than it does in English. In the Greek it means to "cast out" or "thrust out."

- There should be an inner drive in the people that God sends to the field to reap the harvest and to see souls saved.
- Prayer is a foundation for the expression of compassion and the gift of souls.
- There is nothing that we as humans can do except cooperate with God when he sends us or others into the harvest.
- Every Christian, because he is enjoying the benefits of a relationship with God, should be willing to cooperate with God so that others can also enjoy the benefits of walking with Christ.

CONCLUSION:

It is the work of the Holy Spirit that will turn the tide and bring many folks into the kingdom of God. In the meantime, we, as members of Christ's body, can practice being compassionate, communicative, and cooperative. We have the delightful opportunity not only to reap the harvest but to practice on each other until the time comes for us to enter the field.

NOTES:

36

THREE DIMENSIONS OF
SPIRITUAL GROWTH

Text: *²⁸So we continue to preach Christ to each person, using all wisdom to warn and to teach everyone, in order to bring each one into God's presence as a mature person in Christ.* **Colossians 1:28 (NCV)**

INTRODUCTION:

Christianity is not about getting saved and then staying a baby Christian until you die. The emphasis in the text is that Christians must grow and mature. Not only was spiritual growth important to Paul, but Peter also desired to see Christians mature when he said: *²As newborn babies want milk, you should want the pure and simple teaching. By it you can grow up and be saved, ³because you have already examined and seen how good the Lord is.* **1 Peter 2:2-3 (NCV)** The question I will try to answer in this sermon is what is spiritual growth and how do we in fact grow up so that we are fully mature when we meet the Lord? There are three dimensions of spiritual growth that need to be understood and applied to your life if you want to mature in Christ.

PERSONAL SPIRITUAL GROWTH:

The physical universe is an incredibly vast place, and the more we get to know about it the more mind-numbing it becomes. You and I are like tiny little atoms embedded in the fabric of the universe. We have no great value or significance.

- The Bible illustrates this by comparing us to the grass of the field. For example, Peter quotes the Old Testament and says: *²⁴The Scripture says, "All people are like the grass, and all their glory is like the flowers of the field. The grass dies and the flowers fall,* **1 Peter 1:24 (NCV)**

- As enormous as the universe is, and as inconsequential as we are, you and I know a secret that changes everything. The secret is that the maker of this incredible universe knows us and cares for us because he loves us.
- This caring God, this loving God is found in both testaments, but it is never so boldly declared than in the words of John when He said: *[16]"God loved the world so much that he gave his one and only Son so that whoever believes in him may not be lost, but have eternal life.* **John 3:16 (NCV)**
- Christ didn't come for nations or governments; he knew that even his nation of Israel would reject him and the Romans would crucify him.
- He did come for individuals, for you and me even though we have no stature, power, wealth, or glory in ourselves.
- Scripture says that to be saved, we must: *[9]If you use your mouth to say, "Jesus is Lord," and if you believe in your heart that God raised Jesus from the dead, you will be saved.* **Romans 10:9 (NCV)**
- Saying Jesus is Lord means that you have a relationship with him in which he is the focus and head of your life.
- Believing in your heart that God raised Jesus from the dead means that you have a living relationship with him, a relationship that is unique, dynamic and changes as you walk with him through your spiritual life. In other words, to grow and mature spiritually you must have a living relationship with him which is advanced as follows:
  1. By praying to him. All that means is that you talk with him daily.
  2. Meditating on the Word. Since the Holy Spirit speaks to you through the Word, this is a way of listening to what Jesus is saying to you.
  3. By allowing him to change your life. Allowing change is how you respond to your relationship with Him

GROWTH IN THE BODY OF CHRIST:

Some Christians reject the church because they feel that their personal spiritual life is enough. Some reject because they got emotionally offended or hurt in the church. Some reject because they find little or no relevance in the church. Scripture gives us a few reasons why Christians need to belong to a church to mature.

THE BENEFIT OF MEETING TOGETHER:

[25]You should not stay away from the church meetings, as some are doing, but you should meet together and encourage each other. Do this even more as you see the day coming. **Hebrews 10:25 (NCV)**

- It is a primary goal of a healthy church to encourage you to continue the tough process of growing up.
- Only in the church will you find others going through much the same thing that you may be experiencing.
- The church then should be your support group which keeps up your spirit and helps you stay focused on God.

THE CHALLENGE OF MEETING TOGETHER:

[3]You are still not spiritual, because there is jealousy and quarreling among you, and this shows that you are not spiritual. You are acting like people of the world. **1 Corinthians 3:3 (NCV)**

- A healthy church is a place where your immaturity will be exposed. You will have a chance to love the unlovable, and to reject worldly emotions such as jealousy, divisiveness, and quarreling.
- The single most important part of spiritual maturity in the church is that you will be able to love everyone, regardless if you like them, appreciate them, or admire them. Like the church, you must be known for your love.
- Remember that the path to spiritual maturity in the church is to find ways to love as Jesus loved.

THE POWER OF MEETING TOGETHER:

[20]For where two or three come together in my name, there am I with them. **Matthew 18:20 (NIV)**

- The single most important reason for attending church is to meet with Jesus.
- When you worship, hear the Word, and love each other, you get blessings in a way that can't happen in your personal spiritual life.

- In a healthy church, you are lifted up to be with Christ because the Holy Spirit manifests him in unique and individual ways.
- As a result, you are strengthened, empowered, and encouraged to keep Christ in your life.

GROWTH IN SERVICE TO CHRIST:

⁴There are different kinds of gifts, but they are all from the same Spirit. ⁵There are different ways to serve but the same Lord to serve. ⁶And there are different ways that God works through people but the same God. God works in all of us in everything we do. ⁷Something from the Spirit can be seen in each person, for the common good. **1 Corinthians 12:4-7 (NCV)**

God has empowered us to do good works by serving others. To reject service is to reject the primary way that you can grow into a mature Christian. Service is the practical application of your faith in Christ, and without service, you are Christian in name only. James made that clear when he said: *¹⁴My brothers and sisters, if people say they have faith, but do nothing, their faith is worth nothing. Can faith like that save them? ¹⁵A brother or sister in Christ might need clothes or food. ¹⁶If you say to that person, "God be with you! I hope you stay warm and get plenty to eat," but you do not give what that person needs, your words are worth nothing. ¹⁷In the same way, faith that is alone—that does nothing—is dead.* **James 2:14-17 (NCV)**

- Remember that service means work and work calls for sacrifice.
- Sacrifice is a clear means of expressing love for others, and the more loving you become, the more you mature.

CONCLUSION:

Not everyone desires to grow. If we want to be well balanced and mature Christians, we may need to invest more of our time and energy in our weakest areas of growth. We can move from weakness to strength if we look at ourselves honestly and make the necessary corrections to our course. Remember these principles:

- Strive for more intimacy with Christ in prayer, the Word, and submission to his will.

- Strive to be integrated, loyal, faithful, and true to your church. God sent you there for you to mature.
- Strive to find the ministry that God wants you to serve. It doesn't have to be glamorous, just loving.

NOTES:

37
HIGHER GROUND

Text: *¹Since you were raised from the dead with Christ, aim at what is in heaven, where Christ is sitting at the right hand of God. ²Think only about the things in heaven, not the things on earth. ³Your old sinful self has died, and your new life is kept with Christ in God. ⁴Christ is our life, and when he comes again, you will share in his glory. ⁵So put all evil things out of your life: sexual sinning, doing evil, letting evil thoughts control you, wanting things that are evil, and greed. This is really serving a false god. ⁶These things make God angry. ⁷In your past, evil life you also did these things. ⁸But now also put these things out of your life: anger, bad temper, doing or saying things to hurt others, and using evil words when you talk. ⁹Do not lie to each other. You have left your old sinful life and the things you did before. ¹⁰You have begun to live the new life, in which you are being made new and are becoming like the One who made you. This new life brings you the true knowledge of God.* **Colossians 3:1-10 NCV)**

INTRODUCTION:
Most of us would agree that we are too preoccupied with the things of the world. Worldly issues take our time and energy. Mostly we deal with problems, and as we become more involved with the standards and values of the world, we find ourselves in bondage to bad habits. We also find ourselves distant from the life of Christ. In this sermon, I want to look at what Scripture says about looking toward heaven and the impact that it can have in our daily lives.

THINGS IN HEAVEN:
We are instructed by this Scripture to focus our attention on things in heaven. If we pay attention to the things in heaven we can avoid

some serious errors of judgment in our Christian lives. For example, by keeping our eyes turned towards heaven we will find that:

- We are not to be bound by the flesh or social views and limitations which are of the world.
- We must be subject only to Christ.
- Evil surrounds us in the world, and we must remember that the Church is not the world and resist temptations to make it like the world.
- We should be aware that It is dangerous to bring the world into our lives and church.

When we set our minds on the things of Christ, he is welcome to manifest himself in glory through the Holy Spirit. When the church focuses on the world, the Holy Spirit is rejected.

BAD HABITS:

Paul lists some of the sins we must remove from the church and our lives. They are:

1. Sensualism. We focus on feelings, attitudes, opinions, thoughts, and pleasure-seeking.
2. Pride. We think more of ourselves and negatively judge others
3. Division. Unresolved conflicts that cause dissensions, offenses, jealousy, and anger.

God wants you to put off these habits so that you can live a renewed life. God does not want these habits in the church so that we may see and experience his glory. You should have no distractions from the truth of Christ.

GOOD THINGS ABOUT THE NEW LIFE:

God has chosen you and made you his holy people. He loves you. So always do these things:

- Show mercy to others, be kind, humble, gentle, and patient.
- Get along with each other and forgive each other.
- If someone does wrong to you, forgive that person because the Lord forgave you.
- Let the peace that Christ gives control your thinking because you were all called collectively in one body to have peace.
- Always be thankful.

Do all these things; but most importantly, love each other! Love is what holds us all together in perfect unity.

The Christ Life:

How do we begin to live the Christ life? We adopt the characteristics of the Christ. We get the opportunity to acquire those characteristics in the church by;

1. Study of the Word.
2. Through the interaction (pleasant and unpleasant) with other members of the church.
3. By serving the Lord to help fulfill the vision and purpose of the church.
4. By opening ourselves in submission to the work of the Holy Spirit in ourselves and other members of the church.

[17]Everything you do or say should be done to obey Jesus your Lord. And in all you do, give thanks to God the Father through Jesus. **Colossians 3:17 (NCV)** is a great motto for your life in the church.

Conclusion:

When we keep our focus on heavenly things and model our lives after Jesus, we find ourselves delivered from the things that preoccupied us in the world. Keeping our eyes on Jesus ultimately gives us the reward of the Christ life.

Notes:

38

GOD'S VIEW OF YOU

Text: *¹⁰So now I am sending you to the king of Egypt. Go! Bring my people, the Israelites, out of Egypt!" ¹¹But Moses said to God, "I am not a great man! How can I go to the king and lead the Israelites out of Egypt?"* **Exodus 3:10-11 (NCV)**

¹Then Moses answered, "What if the people of Israel do not believe me or listen to me? What if they say, 'The LORD did not appear to you'?" **Exodus 4:1 (NCV)**

¹⁰But Moses said to the LORD, "Please, Lord, I have never been a skilled speaker. Even now, after talking to you, I cannot speak well. I speak slowly and can't find the best words." **Exodus 4:10 (NCV)**

INTRODUCTION:

God gave Moses a task to perform. Granted, it was an impossible task for one man because Moses would have to face the might of the King of Egypt and all the forces that he could muster. Several times during his discussion with God, Moses made excuses for not doing what God wanted him to do. The question is, why did Moses give excuses to God instead of obedience? A lot of the reason is that Moses had a poor self-image. In this sermon, I want to discuss how self-image can impact our service to God.

NOT GREAT:

Moses probably thought that God should send an angel or a king to deal with the King of Egypt. After all, should not a king confront a king? God didn't see it that way, and Moses could not understand why God wanted him to go.

- Moses evaluated worth and ability by social status. In his mind, a humble shepherd could not persuade a king.
- God evaluates the worth of a person by the content of the heart, willingness to serve, and capacity to love.
- It is critical to understand that God will call you to serve him regardless of your status in society or the church. He will call you to help him because of who you are rather than who others think you are.

You cannot refuse to serve God because you think you are not powerful enough, wealthy enough, or admired by others. If God calls you, then you are significant enough in his estimation to serve him.

REJECTION:

Moses believed that the people would reject him because they could not believe that God sent him to bring about their deliverance from Egypt.

- Moses was refusing to serve God because his fear of rejection by the people was greater than his fear of God. By fearing God, I mean having faith that God can overcome any obstacle because he holds all power and authority.
- Godly fear is respecting the divine nature of God. To fear God is to behold his glory and comprehend that his greatness is beyond anything that humanity can achieve.
- Moses' lack of understanding and faith in God, almost caused him to lose the ministry that God set aside for him.
- Moses had to realize that when God called him to deliver Israel, then God would equip and empower him to finish the task set before him.

When God calls us to a ministry, then God will also support, provide, and empower us to do what he called us to do. Unless we believe that God will help us, then we cannot think we will succeed in ministry. Instead, we fear that we may fail and our ministry rejected.

IN OUR WEAKNESS:

In a final attempt to avoid doing what God asked him to do, Moses excused himself because he was a poor communicator. He said that he was slow of speech and could not find the right words to explain what God wanted him to say. Moses implied that this handicap remained even after talking to God.

- We all have handicaps of different types, but those handicaps will have an impact only to the degree that we allow.
- If God thought that our handicap would cause us to fail, he would not have called us in the first place.
- Handicaps are not the criteria to judge our ability.
- With God in our ministry, we can overcome, compensate, or eliminate our handicaps.
- It is excellent news that God is able even when we are disabled.

We are subject to all kinds of handicaps, from a physical problem to old age. God does not call based on a lack of impediments. Instead, he calls us to show that he will overcome our disabilities because in our weakness he shows his power.

CONCLUSION:

Every Christian has a ministry through which he can serve God. Sometimes he asks us to do something that seems impossible. We look at ourselves and believe that we cannot do what he wants and so we invent reasons not to obey. Because we think so little of ourselves, and even less of God, we give him excuse after excuse. The real problem is not acknowledging that with God all things are possible. God's view of us is often better than our self-image, and our self-image needs to conform to God's perspective.

NOTES:

39

THE ANOINTING AND THE CHURCH

Text: [30]*"I can do nothing alone. I judge only the way I am told, so my judgment is fair. I don't try to please myself, but I try to please the One who sent me.* **John 5:30 (NCV)**

[17]*asking the God of our Lord Jesus Christ, the glorious Father, to give you a spirit of wisdom and revelation so that you will know him better.* [18]*I pray also that you will have greater understanding in your heart so you will know the hope to which he has called us and that you will know how rich and glorious are the blessings God has promised his holy people.* **Ephesians 1:17-18 (NCV)**

INTRODUCTION:

The "anointing" is the power of God manifesting through the actions of the Holy Spirit. Walking in the anointing is the authority and the power of Christ acting as a foundation for your daily life. It is walking with Jesus day by day. Unless you learn to walk in the anointing, life can become a burden as the years go by and you have an increase in your sorrows. The good news is that both the Old and the New Testaments promise us that if we walk with God and identify with Jesus who is within us, we will be made free of the stresses and strains of life through the anointing power of the Holy Spirit. (John 16:33) In this sermon, I want to discuss some fundamental principles required to walk in the anointing of God through the Holy Spirit.

OBEDIENCE AND SUBMISSION:

The first principle of great importance is that we must learn to be obedient. In the first text for today, Jesus said that he does "nothing alone." What he was saying is that he was obedient to the will of the Father. The power of the Holy Spirit was directed by the Father's will which Jesus always did to please his Father. For us to work in the anointing at the same level of obedience and submission, we must understand several things about the Lord and the will of the Father. These things are:

- We must understand what the Father likes and what the Father does not like.
- We must understand what he wants us to do and what he expressly forbids us to do.
- We must understand when he wants us to stay or when he wants us to leave.
- We must understand what character traits he wants us to grow into, and what character faults he wants us to change.

The degree of your obedience and submission to Jesus will determine your relationship with him, and the extent to which you walk in his powerful anointing. Keep in mind the following two facts:

1. Partial obedience or submission will produce a superficial relationship and little anointing.
2. Passionate obedience and submission will produce a relationship on fire with the anointing of the Holy Spirit.

SEPARATION OR HOLINESS:

The New Testament encourages us to separate ourselves from the world. An example from the New Testament is: [17] *"Leave those people, and be separate, says the Lord. Touch nothing that is unclean, and I will accept you."* **2 Corinthians 6:17 (NCV).**

- To be holy means that you separate from the evil things of the world. The Holy Spirit is holy, and so his power is also holy.
- Someone stained with a lifestyle of sin in the world will not likely walk in the anointing of the power of the Holy Spirit. The Holy Spirit may give that person a period of time to confess and repent, but ultimately the anointing will leave that person because of his sin.

- The holiness of the Word, the church, and the anointing are all interrelated. Jesus died to fulfill the prophecies of the Word, and to establish his holy church. So how do we leave the world except by cleaving to the local church?
- Personal holiness develops in a church which separates us from the world and its values and temptations.
- I am not just talking about attending a church but becoming an active member of the body of Christ. That means that through the church you are striving to become holy, an acceptable servant of God, and a person of supernatural power.

Two additional facts to keep in mind as you think about your church are:

1. A superficial relationship with your church produces an equally superficial relationship with Jesus and little anointing.
2. God will not force you to become actively committed to his local church, but he wants you to do so because it pleases him.

It is the place where you can begin to learn to be obedient and submitted. So, it is your choice to please God or not. You must also understand that he wants you to submit to those he has appointed as shepherds over you in the church.

CONCLUSION:

I hope that you can see God's purpose and plan that he has for you and the church. The powerful anointing of the Holy Spirit is for you today so that you can bless others in the name of Jesus for the common good of all. That blessing can take place individually as you work with a gift of the Holy Spirit, or it can take place corporately through your church. Keep in mind that the church is the place that you can truly experience the fullness of the anointing of the Holy Spirit, because *"the church is filled with Christ, and Christ fills everything in every way."* **Ephesians 1:22 – 23 (NCV)**

NOTES:

40

WASHING FEET

ext: ¹ It *was just before the Passover Feast. Jesus knew that the time had come for him to leave this world and go to the Father. Having loved his own who were in the world, he now showed them the full extent of his love. ² The evening meal was being served, and the devil had already prompted Judas Iscariot, son of Simon, to betray Jesus. ³ Jesus knew that the Father had put all things under his power, and that he had come from God and was returning to God; ⁴ so he got up from the meal, took off his outer clothing, and wrapped a towel around his waist. ⁵ After that, he poured water into a basin and began to wash his disciples' feet, drying them with the towel that was wrapped around him. ⁶ He came to Simon Peter, who said to him, "Lord, are you going to wash my feet?" ⁷ Jesus replied, "You do not realize now what I am doing, but later you will understand." ⁸ "No," said Peter, "you shall never wash my feet." Jesus answered, "Unless I wash you, you have no part with me." ⁹ "Then, Lord," Simon Peter replied, "not just my feet but my hands and my head as well!" ¹⁰ Jesus answered, "A person who has had a bath needs only to wash his feet; his whole body is clean. And you are clean, though not every one of you." ¹¹ For he knew who was going to betray him, and that was why he said not every one was clean. ¹²When he had finished washing their feet, he put on his clothes and returned to his place. "Do you understand what I have done for you?" he asked them. ¹³ "You call me 'Teacher' and 'Lord,' and rightly so, for that is what I am. ¹⁴ Now that I, your Lord and Teacher, have washed your feet, you also should wash one another's feet. ¹⁵ I have set you an example that you should do as I have done for you. ¹⁶ I tell you the truth, no servant is greater than his master, nor is a messenger greater than the one who sent him. ¹⁷ Now that you know these things, you will be blessed if you do them* **John 13:1-17 (NIV)**

INTRODUCTION:

If you knew that you are going to die in a few days or a few hours, what message would you leave with your family and friends? As we read this Scripture, we catch a glimpse of the message that Jesus wanted his followers to remember and implement. Like the great teacher that he was, he not only told his disciples his message on a verbal level, but he also illustrated it, so they had a living example of what he expected from them and us. There are several messages in these Scripture portions, and I'd like to examine those messages in this sermon.

HIS LOVE:

Jesus had full knowledge of what was about to happen to him. He voluntarily became the Lamb of God offered as a sacrifice for the forgiveness of our sins. What he did as he washed the feet of the apostles was to show the fullness of his love for them by preparing them for their mission once he returned from death. The primary motivation of Christ in this situation was to love his disciples by demonstrating the role they should take in the world.

HIS COMPASSION:

Christ is our master and Lord. He knew too that he was going to return to his Father and seated at his Father's right hand, which is a position of authority and power. (Romans 8:34)

- Given this glorious status to which he was to return, the message he wanted his disciples to learn was that of humility and service.
- The washing of feet was something that a lowly servant would do for his master. The servant washed his master's feet because they had constant contact with the dirt and dust of the world.
- Symbolically, this means that our spiritual feet are always walking in a world of sin, corruption, and temptation. As a result, our spiritual feet get dirty and burdened with the cares and failings of the world.
- Jesus wants us to walk through the world to spread the gospel. And what he demonstrated to his disciples and us, is that he would be there for us when we become weary and burdened by the sinfulness of the world. He showed us that there was nothing we experience in service to him that he doesn't care

about, no matter how trivial it might seem to us, including living in the world stained darkly by sin.

- Another message of Christ when he washed the feet of his disciples, was that he cared about them and loved them enough to keep them pure and clean in a filthy world and that he will do the same for us as we spread the gospel.

THE IMPORTANCE OF HUMILITY:

When Jesus washed the feet of his disciples, he set aside his status and his glory to demonstrate the need for humility on the part of his followers. Peter rejected that humility because it was incompatible with his pride. Many of us do the same thing because we are under the false assumption that humility is equal to weakness. Jesus's insistence that he washed the feet of Peter accomplished three purposes:

1. It communicated the message that there is no one too good to wash the feet of someone else. In other words, if someone needs help, give it to them regardless of their role or status in society or the church.
2. It also communicated the message that no one is so bad or dirty that their feet cannot be washed. In other words, if you need help, then ask for help.
3. Finally, the last message is that no matter who you are, eventually you're going to need help from your Christian brothers and sisters

CONCLUSION:

It's up to us to help each other as we spread the Gospel of the Lord Jesus Christ by walking with the Holy Spirit through a dirty and dusty world. Jesus set us an example, and then he gave us a command to help each other, that is, as he does for us, we need to do for each other. His example, of washing his disciples' feet, has greater meaning than a simple ritual, it is the essence of Christian love for him and each other.

NOTES:

41

ADVENT

Text: *42 "So always be ready, because you don't know the day your Lord will come. 43Remember this: If the owner of the house knew what time of night a thief was coming, the owner would watch and not let the thief break in. 44So you also must be ready, because the Son of Man will come at a time you don't expect him.* **Matthew 24:42-44 (NCV)**

INTRODUCTION:
Advent is a word taken from the Latin word meaning "coming." It is a time of expectation, waiting, and preparation for the coming of Messiah. It has two primary viewpoints:
1. It anticipates the second coming of Christ.
2. It anticipates the birth of Christ.

THE BALANCE:
These two viewpoints are balanced during Advent by how we celebrate the four weeks before Christmas:
- The first two weeks focus on the prophecies of the coming of Christ.
- The second two weeks focus on the Christmas season and the incarnation of Christ.

THE CHURCH AND ISRAEL:
Israel did not accept Jesus during his first coming. They rejected the one who initially came to save the world from the power of sin. They are waiting for the arrival of the Messiah in governing power and authority. The Church accepts the first appearance of the Messiah, and like the Jews, they are now waiting for him to return as the Lord and King of the Earth.

ADVENT LOVE:

The dynamic that drives both the first and second coming is love. Scripture says that: *[16]God loved the world so much that he gave his one and only Son so that whoever believes in him may not be lost, but have eternal life.* **John 3:16 (NCV)**

[3]After I go and prepare a place for you, I will come back and take you to be with me so that you may be where I am. **John 14:3 (NCV)**

ADVENT JOY KILLERS:

If we are not mindful of things that can kill the joy of Advent, we may find ourselves without the Joy due the season. Here are a few things that can kill our joy.

- Materialism: A focus on Christmas gifts will kill joy. It is not what you get but what he gave.
- Stress & Conflicts: Handling Christmas obligations can kill joy because of stress. Keep the season a time of reflection.
- Grief: Not just grief about personal loss, but also about the state of the world can kill joy. This sin-stained world can bring much unhappiness.

CONCLUSION:

While we celebrate Advent every year, we should always remember the benefits we gain from worshipping him as we anticipate his second coming. Just a few of these benefits are:

1. A pathway to God through the forgiveness of our sins.
2. A union with God through the Holy Spirit and the new creation.
3. A certainty that we have eternal life. Not just eternal existence, but the life of God with us, on us, and in us.

NOTES:

42

CHRISTMAS JOY

Text: ¹⁰The *angel said to them, "Do not be afraid. I am bringing you good news that will be a great joy to all the people.* **Luke 2:10 (NCV)** *⁸That night, some shepherds were in the fields nearby watching their sheep. ⁹ Then an angel of the Lord stood before them. The glory of the Lord was shining around them, and they became very frightened. ¹⁰ The angel said to them, "Do not be afraid. I am bringing you good news that will be a great joy to all the people. ¹¹ Today your Savior was born in the town of David. He is Christ, the Lord.* **Luke 2:8-11 (NCV)**

USAGE OF JOY:

Word in Hebrew is Kara:

English Words used in the KJV:

Joy	51
Gladness	3
Joyful	1
joyous	1
Joyfulness	1
Joyfully	1
Greatly	1

[Total Count: 59]

DIFFERENCES BETWEEN JOY AND HAPPINESS:

- Happiness comes from outside events or objects. I.e., I just got a new TV, and I am happy with it.
- Joy comes from a spiritual experience or event. I.e., a fruit of the Spirit is Joy.

CONDITIONS OF HAPPINESS AND JOY:

- You can be happy and joyful at the same time: I am happy that I got a new TV and I feel joyful that God provided for me to get it.
- You can be happy, but not joyful: I am happy that I got a new TV, but I had to pay a lot of money to get it.
- You can be joyful, but not happy: I am unhappy because I am sick now, but I am joyful because God will heal me.

THE SHEPHERDS:

In the Book of John, Jesus said: [11] *I am the good shepherd, and the good shepherd gives up his life for his sheep.* **John 10:11 (NCV).** Jesus identified himself as a shepherd.

- The first public announcement of the birth of Christ was not to kings or religious leaders, but to others like Jesus – shepherds in the field tending their flocks.
- Another word meaning for shepherd is a pastor – so the birth announcement of the Pastor of the World was to other pastors tending their flock.

THE MANIFESTATIONS:

There were three manifestations to these shepherds, which pointed to the supernatural event taking place at the birth of Christ.

1. An angel stood before them: Another word used is a "messenger" who brings good news or tidings. Note he stood before them, i.e., had his feet on the ground not flying in the air. The Scripture does not mention wings, but this angel was a simple messenger.
2. The Glory: The meaning can be brightness and is connected with praise and worship. The very apparent manifestation of the character of God.
3. The Fear: Fear is a natural reaction to the manifest presence of God through the supernatural. Not fear of punishment or destruction, but exceeding reverence.

THE ANNOUNCEMENT:

Do not be afraid: A frequent and common command also made by the Lord at least five times. Can be translated as "alarmed." The command intended to ease anxiety as to what was happening to them by this invasion of the supernatural in their lives.

- Good news: The meaning of the Gospel – the birth of Christ was the beginning of the Gospel – the Good News.
- Great joy: The entire Gospel, but particularly the work of Christ to bring us salvation is joy without end. Regardless of how happy or unhappy we feel at any given time, we all have the foundation of joy that he has saved us, that we belong to him, and that he belongs to us. This is the essential characteristic of Christmas. Not only can we have a "Happy Christmas" but we can also have a "Joyful Christmas." Happy because of the gift of Christ, and joyful because of our relationship with him.
- To all the people: This is prophetic. Not only to all the people of Israel but to all the people of the whole world. The gift of Christ was given to all and can be accepted by everyone.
- Savior and Lord: The functional nature of Christ is that he will save you from the destruction of your sin, and he will guide you and help you live a life pleasing to God. He is your redeemer but also your objective, your ticket out of sin, but also the road you must follow in life.

CONCLUSION:

As we enter the Christmas season, we may be having things happen to us or to someone we love which bring unhappiness into our lives. Even in the mist of that unhappiness, we can experience Christmas joy if we remember the Good News brought by the angel. We have a wellspring of joy in the Lord. Let us rejoice in the gift of Christ and in what he has done for us.

NOTES:

43

NEW YEAR JOY

Text: *⁴We write this to you so you can be full of joy with us.* **1 John 1:4 (NCV)**
⁴Be full of joy in the Lord always. I will say again, be full of joy. **Philippians 4:4 (NCV)**

INTRODUCTION:

Joy is a unique gift given to Christians because of the work of Christ on the cross for the forgiveness of our sins. We can look forward to the coming year and expect it to be joyful. We must understand a few concepts about Christian joy. For example, joy and happiness are two different conditions obtained in different ways.

- Happiness is conditional depending on the situation and your actions,
- Joy is an impartation from the Holy Spirit as a fruit depending on your relationship with Him.

The Lord wants you to be happy but promises that you can be full of joy in the coming year. Let's look at seven sources of joy in the Spirit.

THE JOY OF REDEMPTION:

Elizabeth said ²⁵"Look what the Lord has done for me! My people were ashamed of me, but now the Lord has taken away that shame." **Luke 1:25 (NCV)**

You can become happy by changing your lifestyle. Joy only comes with the realization that God has taken away the shame and sin of your past.

- The joy of redemption is a constant as we remember who we were and who we are now.

- We can experience this joy with each day of the year.

THE JOY OF BLESSINGS:

[46]Then Mary said, "My soul praises the Lord; [47]my heart rejoices in God my Savior, [48]because he has shown his concern for his humble servant girl. From now on, all people will say that I am blessed, [49]because the Powerful One has done great things for me. **Luke 1:46-49 (NCV)**

This verse tells us that we can be joyful just because we know the Lord, and more importantly because he knows us.
- A great God will do great things for us just because he loves us and wants to be our savior.
- In the coming year, we can expect to see such "love miracles" as God intervenes in the world on our behalf.

THE JOY OF VICTORY:

[17]When the seventy-two[£] came back, they were very happy and said, "Lord, even the demons obeyed us when we used your name!" [18]Jesus said, "I saw Satan fall like lightning from heaven. [19]Listen, I have given you power to walk on snakes and scorpions, power that is greater than the enemy has. So nothing will hurt you. [20]But you should not be happy because the spirits obey you, but because your names are written in heaven." **Luke 10:17-20 (NCV)**
- God is not only all-powerful, even against demons and the Devil, but he is on our side.
- That means we can have the joy of victory over what the Devil would bring against us.

THE JOY OF COMMUNITY:

[46]The believers met together in the Temple every day. They ate together in their homes, happy to share their food with joyful hearts. **Acts 2:46 (NCV)**

You are not alone in the world. Christ is in you, but he is also in others like you.
- You can have the joy of a Christian family, and your immediate family can also have joy.
- Participation in the church family will bring joy because the Spirit of God leads the church and resides in your brothers and sisters in the Lord. We are one family, united by love.

Jerome A. Jochem M.S., M.A.

THE JOY OF THE SPIRIT:

²²But the Spirit produces the fruit of love, joy **Galatians 5:22 (NCV)**
⁸You have not seen Christ, but still you love him. You cannot see him now, but you believe in him. So you are filled with a joy that cannot be explained, a joy full of glory. **1 Peter 1:8 (NCV)**

One of the reasons that joy seems scarce in Christians is because many do not have the Baptism of the Holy Spirit.

- The Baptism of the Holy Spirit strengthens the relationship with the Spirit and increases the intensity of the fruit of the Spirit.
- The Spirit becomes the means of love and faith in Christ. Both produce the gift of joy

THE JOY OF GIVING:

²They have been tested by great troubles, and they are very poor. But they gave much because of their great joy. ³I can tell you that they gave as much as they were able and even more than they could afford. No one told them to do it. ⁴But they begged and pleaded with us to let them share in this service for God's people. ⁵And they gave in a way we did not expect: They first gave themselves to the Lord and to us. This is what God wants. **2 Corinthians 8:2-5 (NCV)**

The Spirit of poverty steals the joy of giving.

- Remember that you are giving to God, not to the pastor or the church.
- Giving to God produces a deep joy that strengthens the desire to give more.

JOY IN PERSECUTION:

²²"People will hate you, shut you out, insult you, and say you are evil because you follow the Son of Man. But when they do, you will be happy. ²³Be full of joy at that time, because you have a great reward waiting for you in heaven. Their ancestors did the same things to the prophets. **Luke 6:22-23 (NCV)**

Can we have happiness in a time of persecution? Joy in a time of suffering? How is this possible?

- It is possible only by faith in his promises.

- We look beyond this world into his kingdom and hold on to the faith that he is aware of and will honor our suffering.

CONCLUSION:

As Christians, we have many types of joy, but only one source. Our joy comes from Jesus Christ our Lord and Savior. In every situation, we can find our joy in him.

NOTES:

44

PALM SUNDAY

Text: *⁹ Rejoice greatly, people of Jerusalem! Shout for joy, people of Jerusalem! Your king is coming to you. He does what is right, and he saves. He is gentle and riding on a donkey, on the colt of a donkey.*
Zechariah 9:9 (NCV)

¹²The next day a great crowd who had come to Jerusalem for the Passover Feast heard that Jesus was coming there. ¹³So they took branches of palm trees and went out to meet Jesus, shouting, "Praise^ℓ God! God bless the One who comes in the name of the Lord! God bless the King of Israel!" (Psalm 118:25-26) ¹⁴Jesus found a colt and sat on it. This was as the Scripture says, ¹⁵ "Don't be afraid, people of Jerusalem! Your king is coming, sitting on the colt of a donkey." (Zechariah 9:9) ¹⁶The followers of Jesus did not understand this at first. But after Jesus was raised to glory, they remembered that this had been written about him and that they had done these things to him. ¹⁷There had been many people with Jesus when he raised Lazarus from the dead and told him to come out of the tomb. Now they were telling others about what Jesus did. ¹⁸Many people went out to meet Jesus, because they had heard about this miracle. ¹⁹So the Pharisees said to each other, "You can see that nothing is going right for us. Look! The whole world is following him." ²⁰There were some Greek people, too, who came to Jerusalem to worship at the Passover Feast.
John 12:12-20 (NCV)

³⁹ "'So on the fifteenth day of the seventh month, after you have gathered in the crops of the land, celebrate the LORD'S festival for seven days. You must rest on the first day and the eighth day. ⁴⁰On the first day you will take good fruit from the fruit trees, as well as branches from palm trees, poplars, and other leafy trees. You will celebrate before the LORD your God for seven days.
Leviticus 23:39-40 (NCV)

INTRODUCTION:

We know that on Palm Sunday we celebrate when Jesus entered into Jerusalem as its king. Many preachers pay attention to the circumstances surrounding his procession and the declaration of his kingdom. In this sermon, I intend to preach about what this event meant to Christ.

OUT OF CHARACTER:

During the three-year period of ministry before Palm Sunday, Jesus avoided declaring himself to be a king or the Messiah, nor would he allow others to make that declaration on his behalf. For example:

- Jesus often told his disciples not to tell anyone that he is the Messiah. (Matthew 16:20)
- When Jesus raised the daughter of Jairus, he demanded that his followers do not tell others about the miracle. (Mark 5:43).
- After the transfiguration, he told his disciples that they were not to tell anyone about what they had seen. (Mark 9:9)
- When pressured to reveal himself to the world, he refused to do so. (John 7:4)

From these examples, it is evident that Jesus did not make a public display of himself. He did not hunger for the popular vote of Israel, but in our text for today we see him making a public announcement of his kingship over Israel. The question is why did he change his mind and become a public figure basking in the spotlight of popular culture?

OBEDIENCE IN THE LIGHT OF DISCOMFORT:

While accepting the praise and admiration of the public was foreign to Jesus, following the demands of his Father, and the fulfilling of prophecy was what he desired to do with all his heart. This desire is significant for the following reasons:

- We can see from the Scripture in Zechariah that the king was to enter into Jerusalem while riding a colt.
- In Luke 19 we see that Jesus not only obtained a colt but somehow convinced the owner to loan it to him. Arranging to ride a colt into Jerusalem was the fulfillment of prophecy.

Jerome A. Jochem M.S., M.A.

- Even though participating in a public display was an event that he avoided, he partook in fulfilling prophecy and confirming that Scripture was correct and valid.
- His purpose then was to be obedient to God and had little to do with self-glorification.

Despite his distaste for public adoration, Jesus accepted the accolades of the people of Jerusalem so that the prophetic Word could be completed and perfect in its application. He set aside his preferences to be obedient to his Father.

MIRACLE MAGNATES:

Just before entering into Jerusalem, Jesus had raised Lazarus from the dead. He did this to prove to everyone that he is the resurrection and the life because even the dead respond to his commands.

- Raising Lazarus was just one of many miracles that he did before an astonished public. The long-term effects of the wonders had a lot to do with the size of the crowd and with the attitude of the Pharisees.
- The effect of miracles is accumulative. They were like magnets drawing crowds of people to Jesus so that the people could experience the power and glory inherent in the" wonders."
- Even today, a miracle is a gift of the Holy Spirit. Miracles are "signs" that the kingdom of God is at hand, that the Devil is defeated, and that the name of Jesus is the name of the Almighty God.
- Miracles can also stimulate hatred of God based on jealousy or a sense of competition.
- The Pharisees felt that they were out of control and they feared that people were leaving them.
- This fear resulted in hatred, and they planned to entrap and kill Jesus.
- Every miracle performed by Jesus was for the freedom and healing of people in bondage to Satan. The attitude of the Pharisees reflected the position of Satan.

Jesus encouraged the crowd to believe in miracles because if they believed in miracles, they could understand who he was and what he was about to do to set them free.

Palm Branches:

Palm branches still help us celebrate the Lord. The use of palms in the entry of Jesus into Jerusalem highlights the extreme joy that the people were experiencing because they found their Messiah. Several reasons are noteable:

- The joy the people experienced may have come from the Holy Spirit. Indeed, something motivated the singing of praises and exclamations of kingship expressed to Christ.
- The character of Jesus had a lot to do with their expressions of joy. He was not a threat to them, and that was a blessing since they were living under the cruel rule of Rome. Jesus was both meek and humble and worthy of being the King of Israel.
- The people would turn on Jesus in a few days after his entry into Jerusalem. The hatred of the Pharisees poisoned their hearts, but for now, they shouted blessing on the King

Conclusion:

As we celebrate this Palm Sunday, lets us remember that we have a king who rules with justice, mercy, and compassion. We do not need to fear his rule; we need to rejoice that one day he will return to rule not only spiritually but also physically. All the glory be to God.

Notes:

45

EASTER POWER OF HIS RESURRECTION

TExt: *²⁰ But Christ has indeed been raised from the dead, the firstfruits of those who have fallen asleep. ²¹ For since death came through a man, the resurrection of the dead comes also through a man. ²² For as in Adam all die, so in Christ all will be made alive. ²³ But each in his own turn: Christ, the firstfruits; then, when he comes, those who belong to him. ²⁴ Then the end will come, when he hands over the kingdom to God the Father after he has destroyed all dominion, authority and power. ²⁵ For he must reign until he has put all his enemies under his feet. ²⁶ The last enemy to be destroyed is death.* **1 Corinthians 15:20-26 (NIV)**

INTRODUCTION:

I believe that most of us are more familiar and even comfortable with the passion of Christ than we are with his resurrection. During his passion, he suffered much, but all of us are familiar with suffering. During his passion, he died, but all of us are familiar with death, and many of us have witnessed the passing of a beloved one much to our abundant sorrow. The collective experience is that death is the final point of existence on this earth for the one who is departed. The resurrection of Christ is the exception to this general rule, and because of this, the resurrection is difficult to understand and to comprehend. Even those in the early church doubted the resurrection and were called to an accounting for their lack of faith. So, Paul asked this question: *⁸Why should any of you consider it incredible that God raises the dead?* **Acts 26:8 (NIV)** In this sermon, I'd like to discuss several questions concerning the resurrection of Christ, which will help us to understand its purpose and outcomes.

WHAT IS THE DIFFERENCE BETWEEN BEING RAISED AND RESURRECTED?

In the New Testament, the concepts underlying the terms "being raised from the dead" and being "resurrected from the dead" are interchangeable. For example [12] *But if it is preached that Christ has been raised from the dead, how can some of you say that there is no resurrection of the dead?* **1 Corinthians 15:12 (NIV)**

- There is a distinction between being raised and being resurrected.
- In both the Old and New Testaments, being raised from the dead just meant that the person returned to his old body which was now functional and would eventually die again.
- However, being resurrected from the dead means that an individual has raised from the dead in a body that is significantly different than his old body, in that it has eternal life. This is the resurrection body declared in the New Testament. [42] *So will it be with the resurrection of the dead. The body that is sown is perishable, it is raised imperishable.* **1 Corinthians 15:42 (NIV)**
- Jesus Christ is the only one who raised from the dead in a resurrected body, and that is why he is called the firstfruits. (Vs. 23).

WHO RAISED CHRIST?

In the Old Testament, we see that the prophets occasionally raised someone from the dead. In the New Testament, we know that Jesus raised several people from the dead. (A young girl in Matthew 9, a young man in Luke 7, and Lazarus in John 11) The question is who raised Jesus?

- Scripture tells us that God raised and resurrected Jesus from the dead. [15] *You killed the author of life, but God raised him from the dead. We are witnesses of this.* **Acts 3:15 (NIV)**
- But if we get a little more detailed we find that, in addition to God the Father, both the Holy Spirit ([18] For *Christ died for sins once for all, the righteous for the unrighteous, to bring you to*

Jerome A. Jochem M.S., M.A.

God. He was put to death in the body but made alive by the Spirit, **1 Peter 3:18 (NIV)**) and Jesus Christ himself played a role in his resurrection. [18] *No one takes it from me, but I lay it down of my own accord. I have authority to lay it down and authority to take it up again. This command I received from my Father."* **John 10:18 (NIV)**

- What this means is that all three persons of the Trinity applied Godly power to not only raise Jesus from the dead but also to bring about his bodily resurrection.

WHY WAS HE RAISED?

There are five reasons that Christ was raised in a resurrected body. I will list these as follows:

1. Proof: [4] *and who through the Spirit of holiness was declared with power to be the Son of God by his resurrection from the dead: Jesus Christ our Lord.* **Romans 1:4 (NIV)**
2. Forgiveness of Sin: [17]*And if Christ has not been raised, your faith is futile; you are still in your sins.* **1 Corinthians 15:17 (NIV)**
3. Hope: [19] *If only for this life we have hope in Christ, we are to be pitied more than all men.* **1 Corinthians 15:19 (NIV)**
4. Justification: [25] *He was delivered over to death for our sins and was raised to life for our justification.* **Romans 4:25 (NIV)**
5. Faith: [17] *and if Christ has not been raised, your faith is futile; you are still in your sins.* **1 Corinthians 15:17 (NIV)**

WHAT IS OUR FUTURE?

It is very clear in the New Testament that Jesus promised all those who believe in him a resurrection body and eternal life.

- The promise is that your body will be like his body with all its capabilities, including eternal life. [20] *But our citizenship is in heaven. And we eagerly await a Savior from there, the Lord Jesus Christ,* [21] *who, by the power that enables him to bring everything under his control, will transform our lowly bodies so that they will be like his glorious body.* **Philippians 3:20-21 (NIV)**
- All individuals, believers, and nonbelievers will be raised from the dead to account for their actions. Nonbelievers stand in judgment while believers stand to receive the degree of the award that they accumulated during their lives by doing good. [28] *"Do not be amazed at this, for a time is coming when all who*

are in their graves will hear his voice [29] *and come out--those who have done good will rise to live, and those who have done evil will rise to be condemned.* **John 5:28-29 (NIV)**

- Our resurrection bodies will be glorious and extremely powerful: [43] *it is sown in dishonor, it is raised in glory; it is sown in weakness, it is raised in power;* [44] *it is sown a natural body, it is raised a spiritual body. If there is a natural body, there is also a spiritual body.* **1 Corinthians 15:43-44 (NIV)**

- We will be like Jesus remade in his image and bearing his likeness. [49] And *just as we have borne the likeness of the earthly man, so shall we bear the likeness of the man from heaven.* **1 Corinthians 15:49 (NIV)**

CONCLUSION:

The celebration of Easter is glorious since our Lord and Savior has continued to be with believers, generation after generation because he has risen and is the living and true God. As we celebrate this Easter service, we also celebrate our future in that we can look past the darkness of death into a glorious kingdom promised to us by our Lord and confirmed by the fact that he still lives and moves among us.

NOTES:

46

TAKE UP YOUR CROSS

Text: *³⁸Whoever is not willing to carry the cross and follow me is not worthy of me.* **Matthew 10:38 (NCV)**
²³Then he said to all of them, "If anyone wants to come with me, he must deny himself, pick up his cross every day, and follow me. **Luke 9:23 (NIV)**

²⁷And anyone who does not carry his cross and follow me cannot be my disciple. **Luke 14:27 (NIV)**

INTRODUCTION:

Taking up the cross is not a favorite activity among Christians, especially the "deny yourself" part. We tell others to take up their cross, mostly when we disapprove of their behavior or attitude. Do we know what the cross is and why carrying it daily and continually was so crucial to Christ? We can understand the requirements of the cross if we examine the symbolic, physical, and spiritual meaning of the cross of Christ. The cross has two primary dimensions because every cross has two beams or planks, and each beam tells us what it means to bear our cross daily.

THE VERTICAL BEAM:

The vertical or upright beam is implanted in the earth and points to the heavens.

- The upright beam speaks of your personal, private, and passionate relationship with Jesus.
- The vertical beam concerns no one else but you and Jesus.
- The feet of Christ were nailed to the upright beam.

- Our feet should also be firmly planted on the rock that is Christ: *24 "Everyone who hears my words and obeys them is like a wise man who built his house on rock. 25It rained hard, the floods came, and the winds blew and hit that house. But it did not fall, because it was built on rock.* **Matthew 7:24-25 (NCV)**
- If you were to give a name to the upright beam, it would be the beam of self-discipline.
- Taking up the vertical part of the cross means that you find the time, take time, and spend time with Jesus daily.
  - O Do you worship him by expressing your mutual love?
  - O Do you read the Word to gain knowledge and wisdom about life?
  - O Do you frequently talk with God?
  - O Do you apply the Word to your life situations to live holy lives?
  - O Do you utterly depend on and trust him as you walk with him?
- As incredible as this personal relationship with Christ seems to be, it is not in itself enough for spiritual maturity or balanced spiritual growth. We need the horizontal beam as well.

The Horizontal Beam:
- The horizontal beam does not point up, but it does reach out.
- The horizontal beam speaks of you and others in relationship, both churched and non-churched.
- The hands of Christ that healed the sick touched the untouchable, raised the dead, blessed the children, made the blind see, and expressed his love were nailed to the horizontal beam.
- Without a doubt, the horizontal beam represents the church - the body of Christ reaching out to each other and the lost.

It is evident that every time Jesus reached out a hand, it was to bless in three ways:

3Jesus reached out his hand and touched the man. "I am willing," he said. "Be clean!" Immediately he was cured of his leprosy. **Matthew 8:3 (NIV)**

[25]After the crowd had been thrown out of the house, Jesus went into the girl's room and took hold of her hand, and she stood up. **Matthew 9:25 (NCV)**

Then he touched their eyes and said, "According to your faith will it be done to you";[30] and their sight was restored. **Matthew 9:29-30 (NIV)**

- Taking up the horizontal part of the cross means that you bless others through the church.
- If you have your hands active in the church, then you will make time, take time, and spend time in dedicated service through the church.
  - Do you encourage others by worshipping regularly with them? *[8]So, I want the men everywhere to pray, lifting up their hands in a holy manner, without anger and arguments.* **1 Tim 2:8 (NCV)**
  - Do you handout blessings by active service through the church?
  - Do you reach out to impossible situations with healing hands offering faith and hope?
  - Do you give others a helping hand because of the compassion of Christ?
  - Do you hand over your tithe without counting the cost or expecting a reward?
  - Do you restrain your hands from evil?
- The horizontal beam points to the left and the right, and so includes all of humanity, both lost and saved. It has two parts a left part and a right part - as the criminals on his left and right, we must make a daily decision to follow Jesus or not.

THE WHOLE CROSS:

- The upright beam represents your intimate relationship with Christ.
- The horizontal beam represents your service in the church.
- You must have both to grow correctly.
  - The upright beam without the horizontal results in mysticism and spiritual isolation.
  - The horizontal beam without the upright beam results is social programming and powerless religion.

CONCLUSION:

Only when taken together can you fulfill the great commandment: *[37]Jesus answered, "Love the Lord your God with all your heart, all your soul, and all your mind.' [38]This is the first and most important command.* The first command represents the upright beam pointing to your relationship with God.) *[39]And the second command is like the first: 'Love your neighbor as you love yourself.'* **Matthew 22:37-39 (NCV).** The second command represents the horizontal beam pointing to your service and relationship to others through the church.

NOTES:

47
JULY 4TH - CHRISTIAN FREEDOM

Text: *36So if the Son makes you free, you will be truly free.* **John 8:36 (NCV)**

31So Jesus said to the Jews who believed in him, "If you continue to obey my teaching, you are truly my followers. 32Then you will know the truth, and the truth will make you free." 33They answered, "We are Abraham's children, and we have never been anyone's slaves. So why do you say we will be free?" 34Jesus answered, "I tell you the truth, everyone who lives in sin is a slave to sin. 35A slave does not stay with a family forever, but a son belongs to the family forever. **John 8:31-35 (NCV)**

INTRODUCTION:
Recently, we celebrated the 4th of July. It is a holiday in which we rejoice over the establishment of a democratic republic consisting of free men and women. In fact, it is the time that every person in the colonies became Americans, regardless of their age, race, or origin.

It was a time when everyone had inherent rights and privileges which no government has the authority to take away. It was a time when the world first saw a free nation under God with liberty and justice for all. This nation was born with a heart beating with a passion for freedom. So, today, we must ask the questions necessary to understand freedom and what causes freedom to vanish from the sight of men.

WHAT IS FREEDOM?

- Freedom is not the right to do whatever you want to do when you want to do it. That is anarchy or lawlessness condemned as an error in the Bible: (2 Corinthians 6:14)
- Lawlessness is the enemy of freedom, and we need to be aware and forewarned when our government officials step beyond what the law of the land (the constitution) permits them to do.
- Freedom immerges when a man voluntarily chooses to obey and submit to the law. Not because he must, but because he wants to uphold the standards set before him.
- In a truly free nation, there is room for dissent and even civil disobedience. Everyone must have an equal opportunity to express themselves openly and without fear of retribution.

WHEN IS FREEDOM LOST?

Freedom is lost when obligation, compulsion, or coercion replaces choice. Those under such a harsh rule are referred to as slaves because they have lost their ability to choose their destiny. Freedom can be lost through the action of government, religion, or both combined.

GOVERNMENT:

Freedom is lost when the government is for the politicians by the politicians.

- When the head of government leads based on his desires or whims, then the people suffer a loss of freedom, as they are put under obligation with a penalty of punishment for disobedience.
- Regardless of a politician's intentions, he causes a loss of freedom for the nation when he dictates laws that should be made by the people or the representatives of the people.

RELIGION:

In Christianity, a church or denomination in which grace is minimized, the Holy Spirit is rejected, and men control the body of Christ; legalism will raise its ugly head, and the members will become slaves to the leadership who reinforce a religious dictatorship. Non-Christian religions often stress strict adherence to a literal interpretation of a law, a rule, a religious or moral code, or to a demanding ritualistic practice, and the religious aristocrats become the lords over the life and death of their followers. There seem to be more non-Christian religions which are freedom restricting than Christian churches that can be placed in the same category.

COMBINED:

In my opinion, the perfect example of religion combined with a government that produces a profound lack of freedom is Islam.

- Islam seeks to control every aspect of a person's life and gets embedded in the culture which adopts it.
- Islam is more than just a religion; it is a cultural dictatorship.
- It is legalistic to the extreme, so there is no freedom of religion allowed, and certain classes of people such as women have no liberty at all.
- It is a death religion in that non-believers may be killed in mass. Homosexuals are killed, and women who rebel against family tyrants are killed.

WHAT DID JESUS PROMISE?

In Vs. 36 Jesus said; *So if the Son makes you free.* The word "free" means to liberate. Another concept which fits this word is to deliver from bondage. In the second part of that verse, Jesus said; *you will be truly free.* In this second use of the word "free" it means that a person is unrestrained, that is, he has the status of a citizen and not a slave, or he is exempt from obligation or liability. He is a free man or woman and is at liberty to fulfill his or her destiny.

- Jesus was saying that when he sets you free from your sin life (delivers you from sin) then for the first time you experience genuine liberty and real freedom.
- The people who established our country had a genuine passion for freedom.
- They had experienced religious and political tyranny and wanted nothing to do with it.
- From where did this passion come? They were Christians, and it came from their experience of being set free by Christ.

- Because Christ had set them free, they wanted to live as liberated men and to guarantee that their children would be free as well.

CONCLUSION:

We must remember that men in bondage to sin need to be freed by a saving experience with Christ. We must reach out to those who need him so that they can be "truly free." The most effective way to allow real freedom is to see to it that salvation reigns instead of military force.

NOTES:

48

MEMORIAL DAY SERVICE

T ext: *³⁶So if the Son makes you free, you will be truly free.* **John 8:36
(NCV)**

INTRODUCTION:
Today is the day that we honor those men and women who served in
a military force and died so that our country is secure.

REASONS:
There are a wide variety of reasons that a man or woman would seek
military service when there is no reason such as a mandatory draft.
- Need for appreciation/recognition.
- Need for support for education.
- Need to strike out on his own by getting away from home.
- The deep need for a new start - a new beginning, which only
  the military can give.

But underneath it all, is a sincere desire to protect the freedom of
loved ones. I think this is the most honorable reason to risk death for
the sake of the freedom of others.

WHY DO WE STRIVE AND DIE FOR FREEDOM?
Ironically, we fight and die for freedom because we are born into
slavery of two types.

1). Slavery of Sin:
*³⁴Jesus answered, "I tell you the truth, everyone who lives in sin is a slave to
sin.* **John 8:34 (NCV)**
- We are born into slavery.

- The mark of that birth is called Original Sin and is the inheritance we get from Adam and Eve.
- Given two choices we will always choose the way that leads to captivity.
- Because we cannot help but sin, our master is Satan, and he is a harsh master indeed

2). Slavery of the Law:
We have freedom now, because Christ made us free. So stand strong. Do not change and go back into the slavery of the law. **Galatians 5:1 (NCV)**
When we base our faith on keeping the law, we lose our freedom.
- Not only do we lose our freedom in Christ, but we become slaves to the law.
- In other words, we come into bondage to the law through legalism.

WHAT IS THE SOLUTION?
We have freedom now, because Christ made us free. (Galatians 5:1A).

How did he make us free? Through the cross and death of Jesus for our sins. Christ is the only way we can be free.

Solution to Slavery of the Law:
Christ frees us from the law by giving us a new spirit after we accept him as our Lord and Savior. Note in the above Scripture Paul is telling the Galatians to stand firm by focusing on the freedom given by Christ rather than the bondage of the law.
- Religious bondage always occurs when people take their eyes from Jesus and depend on the rules of their denomination.
- Religious bondage strips away the fullness of what Christ has given us.
- Religious slavery results in demonic bondage as judgementalism and self-righteousness flourishes in the church.

Solution to Slavery of Religion: *15For you did not receive a spirit that makes you a slave again to fear, but you received the Spirit of sonship. And by him we cry, "Abba Father."* **Romans 8:15 (NIV)**

- We are freed from religion because we are not slaves, but children of God.
- The Father treats (sees) us as sons and daughters and not just servants or slaves.
- We are adopted into his family, and we have the rights and privileges of the New Testament.
- The dynamics of our relationship are based on love and not control. We must love each other so that we are all equal and accepted in the church.

Consider the case of Onesimus, who was a slave that robbed Philemon and then came to meet Paul in Rome. Here is what Paul prescribed for this slave and criminal: *[16]no longer as a slave, but better than a slave, as a loved brother. I love him very much, but you will love him even more, both as a person and as a believer in the Lord.* **Philemon 1:16 (NCV)**

This freedom is from the nature of sin. Love cancels all slavery and replaces it with freedom and forgiveness.

CONCLUSION:

Here is a reason we honor those who give up their lives to protect an often rebellious and sinful nation. Like Paul, those who serve by protecting the freedom of the nation are also preserving our love for each other. We have the mute testimony of that love by looking at the rows and columns of headstones in military cemeteries everywhere in our country.

NOTES:

49
FATHER'S DAY

Text: *"This, then, is how you should pray:" 'Our Father in heaven,"*
Matthew 6:9 (NIV)

INTRODUCTION:

The first line of the Lord's Prayer is simple, but it contains a deep
ocean of guidance about how to pray, the Christian community, and
our relationship with the Father God. In this sermon, I would like to
explore just the first part of the Lord's Prayer and to show how the
ideas contained in this verse apply to our prayer life.

PRAYER TYPES:

Jesus instructed his followers how to pray. His instructions stirred up
noteworthy debate among various Christian groups and resulted in
two significant streams of opinion about how Christians should pray:

1. In a specific form. This type of prayer is called ritualized
   prayer. Christian denominations have written entire prayer
   books with prayers that cover a multiple of situations and
   services. Many Christians use these prayers to express their
   collective needs, especially in church services that are highly
   structured and ritualized.
2. In a general context-free form or flowing prayer. When
   Christians need to express deeply felt emotions, or desire to
   have a chat with God, they may say a prayer that reflects their
   feelings and is very personal. When the person is Spirit-filled,
   the prayer may be in tongues.

Both types of prayer are valid, and every person is free to use both
approaches when they pray.

OUR:

The very first word of this Scripture tells us that we belong to a community of Christians. We are not to pray just for ourselves, but for each other. It reveals the Father's heart for his family. The members of which are to be one in his name and his power. The first word reflects the inclusiveness of Christianity. The only qualifier to belong to the Father's family is to believe in Jesus Christ. All other characteristics such as race, gender, age, and geographical location do not limit membership.

OUR FATHER:

He is a father to all humanity by creation. (Acts 17:28) This fatherly concern for everyone is the reason that all of humanity has been offered the path of salvation through Jesus. Jesus wants all humanity to have the option of knowing the Father God.

He is uniquely a father to the saints, by adoption and regeneration. As a result, the following principles apply concerning our prayer to Father God.

1. We are to pray to him and him alone in the name of Jesus.
2. We are to approach him as our father – knowing in our hearts that he will listen to us because he cares for us.
3. We are to respect him and honor him – while he is intimate with us, he remains the Almighty God of the universe.

FATHER GOD:

The title of Father God contains two other spiritual realities which we must recognize:

1. When we use the word "father," we are approaching God with the love that a child has for his father.
2. When we begin to pray to our Father, we express confidence that God will be a father to us regardless of our situation. We are confident that he will show us understanding, mercy, forgiveness, and compassion because he sees us as his children through Christ.

IN HEAVEN:

This phrase reminds us that God is our spiritual father and as such does not share the faults and limitations of our earthly fathers. This phrase also tells us that our Father God in heaven is:

- All powerful.
- Majestic.
- Pure.
- Holy.
- All-knowing.
- Everywhere Present.
- He has Dominion.
- Worthy of adoration.

CONCLUSION:

Jesus told us so very much in just the first part of his prayer. What a wonderful Father we have. We who accept Christ find the Father because we believe. We should pray for each other because we are one in Christ and have the same Father, and we should always keep in mind that we belong to the same family because we have one Father in heaven.

NOTES:

50

MOTHER'S DAY

Text: *⁵ I remember your true faith. That faith first lived in your grandmother Lois and in your mother Eunice, and I know you now have that same faith.* **2 Timothy 1:5 (NCV)**

INTRODUCTION:

Today we are celebrating our mothers on Mother's Day. This holiday, like Father's Day, is like a double-edged sword.

- On the one hand, we want to honor our mothers, and encourage all the mothers in our body to celebrate this day of God's blessing - the blessing of your children. *³ Children are a gift from the LORD; babies are a reward.* **Psalm 127:3 (NCV).** They are those who are blessed.
- On the other hand, we must be sensitive to those women whom God has not blessed with children, even though they might desperately want a child. They are those who wait.
- Finally, there is that group of women who are not married, and they set their hearts on the hope that one day somewhere in the future they will have the children of that wonderful husband that God will send them. They are those who hope.

The heart of this sermon is to explore what the Word has to say to each of these groups of women.

THOSE WHO ARE BLESSED:

¹² "Honor your father and your mother so that you will live a long time in the land that the LORD your God is going to give you. **Exodus 20:12 (NCV)**
As you gave birth to your children, you also experienced a transformation in yourself.

You began to act in two distinct ways:

- First, you felt the love only a mother can feel for her child. It is a love that, like God's love, covers a multiple of sins and offenses.
- Secondly, while you are feeling this beautiful motherly love, you are also developing into a firm disciplinarian and a stern teacher.

Your child separates from you as the child grows older. Your teachings are tested.

- Scripture tells your child to honor your every attempt to raise him up correctly.
- Honoring your mother results in the reward of long and a blessed life, but of most importance, he will have the same faith that you demonstrated to him each time that you loved him and disciplined him.
- The degree to which you blessed him with righteousness, love, and truth is the degree to which he will honor you.
- Paul witnessed that Timothy had the living faith of his mother and grandmother. Nothing more needs to be said about these women who were truly women of God.

THOSE WHO WAIT:

There is nothing quite as painful as wanting a child but not being able to have one. It is a burden and hurt that eventually changes into a sad longing without reprieve.

Scriptures comfort such women by telling them that others have had similar experiences and God blessed them with the desire of their heart. *9 He gives children to the woman who has none and makes her a happy mother. Praise the LORD!* **Psalm 113:9 (NCV)**

Some examples are:

- Sarah: Waited for most of her married life for that baby she so desperately wanted. Eventually, at the age of 90, God gave her a son. When she heard the declaration that she would be pregnant, she laughed, and the Lord told her to call her son "Isaac" which means laughter.

- Hannah: Waited for many years and suffered from both depression and shame because she did not have a child. She said, *"I have many troubles and am very sad"* **1 Samuel 1:16 (NCV)** God heard Hannah's prayers and gave her a son who she named Samuel. Samuel became a great prophet, and yet would not even exist except for Hannah's persistent prayer and faith in God.
- Manoah's Wife: She remains unnamed in Scripture. She lived under the tyranny of the Philistines. She could not have a child until an angel appeared to her with God's promise that she would give birth to a son. She named him Samson, and he was to deliver Israel.
- Elizabeth: She wanted children but couldn't have any, and on top of that she was very old, certainly beyond childbearing age much like Sarah. God gave her a child who became John the Baptist, the forerunner of Jesus Christ.

THOSE WHO HOPE:

[10] It is hard to find a good wife because she is worth more than rubies. [11] Her husband trusts her completely. With her, he has everything he needs. [12] She does him good and not harm for as long as she lives. **Proverbs 31:10-12 (NCV)**

If you are a woman who hopes for marriage and children, then be of good cheer. God certainly will give you that extraordinary man who is already waiting for you.

- God promised that each man who so desires marriage has a mate ready to be with him on the path of life. Scripture tells us that the Lord said: *[18] "It is not good for the man to be alone. I will make a helper who is right for him. "* **Genesis 2:18 (NCV)**
- Remain hopeful and practice becoming "worth more than rubies," by growing close to the Lord while you dream of marriage and children. (Vs. 10)

CONCLUSION

The heartbeat of a good mother is love. No matter how difficult life becomes or how flawed your character, you should always bestow on your children the most precious gift you have to give, unconditional love. It is your love that will be the foundation of his faith because he will be able to relate to God who is love.

NOTES:

51

THANKSGIVING

Text: *¹⁶Always be joyful. ¹⁷Pray continually, ¹⁸and give thanks whatever happens. That is what God wants for you in Christ Jesus.*
1 Thessalonians 5:16-18 (NCV)

INTRODUCTION:
This week we will celebrate Thanksgiving, a uniquely American and Christian Holiday. Spiritually, Thanksgiving represents an essential spiritual principle which can have a significant impact on our daily lives. This principle is so important that God commanded us to be thankful.

I am going to talk about four reasons that we should give thanks to God.

FOUR REASONS TO GIVE THANKS:
1). Giving thanks to God focuses your mind and heart on positive events rather than a preoccupation with the adverse events in your life.

- We can strengthen the grip of negativity in our lives by concentrating on all the hurtful and painful things that happen regardless of our choice.
- As we pay attention to those negative events, we lose sight of the blessings and positive events which are also happening right along with the negative. Our text says that we are to give thanks "whatever happens," and this means that we do not give thanks for the negative, but we find something positive to give thanks for amid all the negative.
- We face a tough choice. We either give attention to the negative and that leads to bondage followed by depression

or we concentrate on the positive by giving thanks to God for his blessings, and that leads to both peace and joy.

2). Giving thanks reveals the nature of God and provides a foundation for a relationship with him.

- People are often puzzled by why bad things happen to good people. Some people eventually blame God for allowing the bad things to happen to them or a loved one, and they get angry enough at God to reject him. They do not seek things in their lives to be thankful for, but they react by rejecting God.
- Of course, we know as Christians that we have an enemy and that enemy is responsible for bad things happening not God
- A more significant mystery and revelation concerns why good things happen to bad people. Jesus said that we are to bless those who curse us and pray for people who are cruel to us. (Luke 6:28)
- The simple fact is that a small act of kindness or goodness can have a profound impact on evil people, even bringing them to salvation.
- When a person returns to God after a hurt, or because of some simple act of goodness, there is great reason to be thankful to our God of love, compassion, and mercy.

3). Giving Thanks cultivates an attitude of gratitude.

- People who believe that they are entirely responsible for their own lives have no reason to be grateful, and therefore they have no appreciation of God.
- People who have surrendered their lives to God understand that all they have and all they are is dependent on God, and so they practice gratitude in every situation. The heart of an "attitude of gratitude" is expressed in this passage: *¹Praise the LORD! Thank the LORD because he is good. His love continues forever.* **Psalms 106:1 (NCV)**

4). Giving thanks becomes a high form of praise and worship which proclaims God's glory and sovereignty. *I will give thee thanks in the great congregation: I will praise thee among much people.* **Psalms 35:18 (NIV).**

- We can thank God for a wide variety of reasons, including giving thanks for each other.
- But in every instance, we glorify God and attract attention to him during our worries and pains.
- We essentially praise him in our thanksgiving, and that speaks volumes to the world about the nature and character of our Lord and Savior.

CONCLUSION:

When we give thanks to God during our problems, we are proclaiming that our hope is in him and that we shall not be disappointed. Inherent in giving thanks is a profound humility, a concession to the truth that God is Lord and King of our lives. Only if we are in our little world will we fail to give thanks for all that he has done for us. Enjoy this Thanksgiving Holiday with food, family, and friendship, but do not forget to give thanks to God.

NOTES:

52

CHRISTIAN MARRIAGE

Text *²¹Yield to obey each other because you respect Christ. ²²Wives, yield to your husbands, as you do to the Lord, ²³because the husband is the head of the wife, as Christ is the head of the church. And he is the Savior of the body, which is the church. ²⁴As the church yields to Christ, so you wives should yield to your husbands in everything. ²⁵Husbands, love your wives as Christ loved the church and gave himself for it ²⁶to make it belong to God. Christ used the word to make the church clean by washing it with water.²⁷He died so that he could give the church to himself like a bride in all her beauty. He died so that the church could be pure and without fault, with no evil or sin or any other wrong thing in it. ²⁸In the same way, husbands should love their wives as they love their own bodies. The man who loves his wife loves himself. ²⁹No one ever hates his own body, but feeds and takes care of it. And that is what Christ does for the church, ³⁰because we are parts of his body. ³¹The Scripture says, "So a man will leave his father and mother and be united with his wife, and the two will become one body. ³²That secret is very important—I am talking about Christ and the church. ³³But each one of you must love his wife as he loves himself, and a wife must respect her husband.* **Ephesians 5:21-33 (NCV)**

INTRODUCTION:

Right from the first verse, this Scripture can trigger a lot of controversies even in the church. The more an individual is ignorant of the Bible as a whole, the easier it is to misrepresent and misuse the Christian principles of unity and success in a Christian marriage found in these Scriptures. For the enemy of the church, these Scriptures have been used to declare Christianity as an anti-feminine, sexually abusive, and sexist religion. Of course, nothing can be furthest from the truth.

To get a balanced understanding of these Scripture verses, you have to keep two factors in mind.

1. Paul's letter to the Ephesian Church was a disciplinary letter. The church was messing up, and Paul needed to stand in his authority and get it straight. Paul had to be frank and commanding in this letter. Paul had no room for politically correct speech, so he is blunt and appears insensitive.

2. Paul was addressing Christian marriages and not secular marriage. There is a significant difference between these types of marriage.

SECULAR MARRIAGE:

Essentially, secular marriage is a legal contract made between two people and the state to determine the distribution of wealth if one person should die or divorce. The key to understanding this type of marriage is that it carries no spiritual dimension with it. It is merely two people living together for the cultural benefits without spiritual commitment or obligation to each other. In our current culture, many people feel that secular marriage is not necessary and so they live together.

CHRISTIAN MARRIAGE:

While Christian marriage is also a legal contract involving the state, its primary purpose is to bring Jesus Christ into the relationship of the married couple. For both parties in a Christian marriage, Jesus is Lord and Savior and is to be considered the third party in their relationship. As a result, married Christians have Christ in them, with them, and upon them resulting in an unlimited and exciting future as a team working on making their marriage better, happier, and long-lasting.

The spiritual component of a Christian marriage far outweighs the legal element of the secular marriage, and the commitment between the couple and Christ creates a team that has unbreakable unity.

THE TEAM:

In Vs. 21, Paul lays the foundation of unity by saying: *21Yield to obey each other because you respect Christ.22Wives, yield to your husbands, as you do to the Lord, ²³because the husband is the head of the wife, as Christ is the head of the church. And he is the Savior of the body, which is the church. ²⁴As the church yields to Christ, so you wives should yield to your husbands in everything.*

God set up Christian marriage as a team. The purpose of the team is to accomplish God's will and so to receive his blessing in the marriage.

- The relationship between the husband and wife is one of respect. Each has a right to speak their mind without fear of punishment. Each person has opinions and solutions that should be discussed and an outcome planned.
- In the eyes of God, the husband and wife are co-equals in their individual ability to contribute to the team.
- The team plan of action is usually the best way to achieve God's will in any given circumstance.
- Every team, if it is at all functional, has a team leader who has the final decision in any team efforts.
- Without a team leader, the team would not reach a conclusive decision and would get caught in an endless loop of conflict.

TEAM AUTHORITY AND SUBMISSION:

God declares the husband to be the team leader, and that the wife should submit to the final decisions made by the husband in the same way the church is to submit to Christ.

- Giving the husband the role of the team leader does not make him into a dictator or imply that he does not need the wise advice and counsel of the wife.
- It does mean that he had better operate in the fullness of his love for his wife and his God. Remember that the team leader must answer to God for the decisions he makes.

²⁵Husbands, love your wives as Christ loved the church and gave himself for it ²⁶to make it belong to God. Christ used the word to make the church clean by washing it with water.²⁷He died so that he could give the church to himself like a bride in all her beauty. He died so that the church could be pure and without fault, with no evil or sin or any other wrong thing in it. (Vs. 25-27)

- The glue that keeps a Christian marriage together is love. The team leader is to love his wife as Christ loved the church.
- The examples of love that Paul talks about in Scriptures are perfect examples of agape. It is this Christ love that builds the necessary unity for the marriage team not only to survive in the world but to overcome it.

CONCLUSION:
28In the same way, husbands should love their wives as they love their own bodies. The man who loves his wife loves himself. (Vs. 28)

As the world draws them away from their families, it is possible for a man or a woman to walk away from the marriage team and become self-centered. Either may forget the love of Christ and the love of Christ found in their mate. This love can be re-established and is waiting for them once they return to the marriage team. Sin is the leading cause of this amazing loss of love for each other. Repentance returns love to their relationship, and often they find a new unity based on forgiveness and trust.

NOTES:

Author Information

Pastor Jerry Jochem has been an ordained pastor for 26 years. He has been with the Assembly of God fellowship for the last nine years. He is presently pastor of Abundant Life Assembly of God in Winchester.

Pastor Jerry has a Master's degree in Psychology from the University of Mississippi and a Master's degree in Bible Studies from Liberty Bible College which was a part of Liberty Fellowship.

In addition to being a pastor, he functions as a counselor for the Family Counseling Center in Winchester, Tennessee.

Pastor Jerry has been happily married to Roxie Jochem for 46 years. Roxie is a licensed minister with the Assemblies of God Fellowship.

Pastor Jerry has written two other e-books. The first book is entitled "The Spirit Universe: A Christian Viewpoint" and is designed to reach out to those in the occult and ghost hunting populations with the message of the Gospel. The second book is entitled "Defeating Cancer: a Christian Spiritual Warfare Model" and originated from the fact that Roxie has been healed of ovarian cancer which re-occurred five times. The Spirit Universe book is being converted to paperback and may be soon published.

Printed in the United States
By Bookmasters